# Time and Eternity

**Classics of Modern Japanese Thought and Culture**

The Ways of Thinking of Eastern Peoples
*Hajime Nakamura*

A Study of Good
*Kitaro Nishida*

Climate and Culture: A Philosophical Study
*Tetsuro Watsuji*

Time and Eternity
*Seiichi Hatano*

Studies in Shinto Thought
*Tsunetsugu Muraoka*

The Japanese Character: A Cultural Profile
*Nyozekan Hasegawa*

An Inquiry into the Japanese Mind as Mirrored in Literature
*Sokichi Tsuda*

About our Ancestors: —The Japanese Family System
*Kunio Yanagita*

Japanese Spirituality
*Daisetz Suzuki*

A Historical Study of the Religious Development of Shinto
*Genichi Kato*

# Time and Eternity

*by*

SEIICHI HATANO

*translated by*

ICHIRO SUZUKI

Assistant Professor

Aoyama Gakuin University

**Greenwood Press**

New York • Westport, Connecticut • London

**Library of Congress Cataloging-in-Publication Data**

Hatano, Seiichi, 1877-1950.
   Time and eternity.

   Translation of: Toki to eien.
   Reprint. Originally published: 1963.
   1. Time.   2. Eternity.   I. Title.
BD638.H313   1988      115      88-21949
ISBN 0-313-26557-7

British Library Cataloguing in Publication Data is available.

© Ministry of Education, Japan, 1963

Library of Congress Catalog Card Number: 88-21949
ISBN: 0-313-26557-7

First published in 1963

Reprinted in 1988 by Greenwood Press, Inc. jointly with
Yushodo Co., Ltd., Tokyo with the permission of the Ministry of
Education, Japan

Printed in the United States of America

The paper used in this book complies with the
Permanent Paper Standard issued by the National
Information Standards Organization (Z39.48-1984).

10 9 8 7 6 5 4 3 2 1

In Memory of My Wife

Dr. Seiichi Hatano (1877–1950)

Unesco, at the 9th session of its General Conference held in New Delhi in 1956, decided to launch the Major Project on Mutual Appreciation of Eastern and Western Cultural Values.

In accordance with the decision, this Commission has been carrying on, since 1958, within the framework of the project, a programme of publishing modern Japanese philosophical works translated into foreign languages.

We have so far brought out the following three books: "The Ways of Thinking of Eastern Peoples" by Hajime Nakamura; "A Study of Good" by Kitaro Nishida; and "A Climate" by Tetsuro Watsuji. The present volume is the fourth of the series.

Dr. Seiichi Hatano is well known as a forerunner of the study of western philosophy among Japanese scholars and his "Time and Eternity", which is the fruit of his deep meditation and profound studies, is recognized as his representative work.

It is hoped that this book will prove useful to those students and scholars who wish to get familiar with Japanese thought.

Our acknowledgement is due to Dr. Ken Ishihara and Dr. Yosuke Hamada for providing us with valuable materials and advice, which enabled us to prepare the introductory note "The Life and Thought of Dr. Seiichi Hatano" contained in the present volume.

*January, 1963*

**Japanese National Commission for Unesco**

# Contents

# The Life and Thought of Dr. Seiichi Hatano

The life of Dr. Seiichi Hatano (1877–1950), one of the pioneers of the study of Western philosophy in Japan and especially that of religion, is roughly divided into two periods which are marked by different approaches to philosophy. The first is an epoque when his concern was more centered in the historical study of Western thought. The second is a period when his own system in the field of the philosophy of religion was gradually constructed. Both of them bequeathed series of books[1] which contributed considerably to the study of occidental philosophy in this country which had been closed to Western culture until the middle of the last century.

When Hatano first started his career as a student of philosophy in 1896 at the University of Tokyo, he met a German philosopher, Dr. Raphael von Koeber.[2] Koeber was a student of Kuno Fischer who wrote *Geschichte der neueren Philosophie* in 1854. It was under the guidance of this German scholar[3] that Hatano's philosophical interest was directed to the historical study of spiritualism starting from ancient

1) Hatano's historical writings are: *Outline of the History of Western Philosophy*, 1901; *The Origin of Christianity*, 1908; *The History of Religious Thoughts of the West*, Vol. I. Greece, 1921; *The Primitive Christianity*, 1950. His three major systematical writings on the philosophy of religion are: *Philosophy or Religion*, 1935; *An Introduction to the Philosophy of Religion*, 1940; *Time and Eternity*, 1943.

2) It was Ludwig Busse who was first invited to teach philosophy in the department of philosophy right after its establishment in the college of liberal arts in 1886. It is said that Busse was a student of Lotze. He stayed for six years in Japan until 1892 when Dr. Koeber replaced him from Munich by the introduction of Eduard von Hartmann.

3) The intimate relationship of the two is reflected in various parts of Hatano's writings. "One of the most unforgetable things in my life is the fact that Dr. Koeber gave me the proper orientation to philosophy in my college days. When I recollect all the changes and development of my thought since, I cannot but feel deep gratitude for what he did for me." (*Complete Works*, Vol. 3)

Greece and extending through the Middle Ages up to German Idealism. Hatano as a young student of philosophy took up the critical philosophy of Kant as a theme while digesting such books on the history of philosophy as those of Kuno Fischer, Zeller, Erdmann, Windelband, Ueberweg and arranging them in a book, *Outline of the History of Western Philosophy* (1901). There had been by that time several introductory books on the history of philosophy in Japanese language. But some of them, as Hatano indicates in the book,[1] were more or less verbal translations of foreign books and their wordings and styles were not very satisfactory. By that time there was still a considerable degree of language barrier. And the want of basic knowledge in Western culture in general had been a great obstacle in almost all the academic fields in Japan. It is surprising that a young Japanese of only 24 years could master German so rapidly, when there were not very good grammars nor dictionaries. In this book Hatano described very clearly and precisely the main current of occidental thought starting from ancient Greece up to the second half of the 19th century including the philosophies of Lotze and Fechner. We know how brilliant he was from the fact not only that the book was an excellent guide to the students of philosophy of that time, but also that even now it is widely used as a textbook at various schools. It should be said that the whole system of his philosophy of religion which was to be constructed in his later years was built on the basis of this wide and deep historical insight into Western philosophy and religion, both Greek and Christian, which was first inspired by Dr. Koeber and then deepened when Hatano was in Germany (1904–1906). It was sometime before he left for Germany that Hatano, while studying at the University of Tokyo, was baptized by the Rev. Masahisa Uemura, one of the leading figures of the early Protestant churches in Japan.

Immediately after this book was published, he concentrated his efforts on completing his doctoral dissertation, *A Study of Spinoza*,[2]

1) Cf. Hatano's preface in his *Outline of the History of Western Philosophy*.
2) It was translated into Japanese by Yoshishige Abe and published by Keiseisha in 1910.

which was written in German in 1904. Then he left Japan for further study in Germany. Although the main theme of his study was the history of spiritualism from Spinoza to German Idealism in relationship to the philosophy of ancient Greece, there a completely new perspective on Christianity and Christian theology was given to him. At the University of Berlin he attended the lectures of Adolf von Harnack and Otto Pfleiderer. At Heidelberg he was guided by Wilhelm Windelband who had succeeded Kuno Fischer and through whom Hatano got acquainted with the Neo-Kantian philosophy. In the field of theology he was much inspired by the lectures of Johannes Weiss, Ernst Troeltsch and Adolf Deissmann. And there at Heidelberg Hatano reconfirmed his view that in the whole spiritual tradition of the West there flows a strong current of Christian philosophy. Soon after his return in 1906, Hatano began to tackle the subjects in this sphere. The subject of his lectures at the University of Tokyo (1907–1908) was *The Origin of Christianity* which was compiled in a book in 1908. At the time when this book was written, he was more attracted to the camp of the Neo-Kantian school which inherited the tradition of German Idealism. Namely, he was driven to the line of thought expressed by Windelband and Troeltsch. He was especially impressed by the interpretation of the latter on the Kantian philosophy of religion.

But Hatano's critical mind was never satisfied with the attitude of the German school to New Testament theology. Seigo Yamaya, Professor of New Testament at Tokyo Union Theological Seminary, describes the point very precisely in the exposition of Hatano's thought[1] in which he states how Hatano did not fall into the defect of the German school, although he was much influenced by it:

> " When we go into the detail of *The Origin of Christianity*, we shall discover an excellent historian and thinker in Hatano quite clearly in the fact that, in spite of the exactitude and thoroughness of his thinking, being quite aware of the limit of rationalism

---

1) Hatano, *The Origin of Christianity* (Kadokawa Bunko), p. 194.

in the interpretation of history, he made his description from a particular aspect of religious experience and without running into the extremity of the *religionsgeschichtliche Schule*, he developed his personal thought very freely exercising his own independent judgment. What he aimed at was, of course, true historical interpretation of events and pursuit of what actually happened in history. But his description was made not simply from an academic interest, but from a sincere consideration of the special feature of religious life as such. Here we find his basic stand which has been developed into his later work on the *Philosophy of Religion*."

Afterwards in the year 1923, he gave similar lectures at the University of Kyôto which were published after his death in 1950.[1] These two books, however, show us the development of Hatano's thought in those fifteen years. In the latter Hatano has gone beyond the point of view of the German school of religious history (*die religionsgeschtliche Schule*) and, from much broader perspective, tried to understand the core of the New Testament religion, often ignoring some of its unessential factors. One can even observe his attempt to step into the analysis of theological issues such as the Pauline conceptions of Christ's death, sacrifice and redemption.

In describing the New Testament religion in this book, Hatano, of course, examined the sources and referred to the textual exegesis of the Bible. To that extent, he owed much of his study to those of the theologians. But further in the explanation of the religious content of the teachings of Jesus and St. Paul, he exercised mainly his original method of understanding the essential meaning of events and history, a method which is often adopted in the study of philosophy. As it is pointed out by Yamaya, Hatano did not remain at

---

1) Hatano, *The Primitive Christianity* (Iwanami Zensho), Tokyo, 1950. In this book, the description of the Fourth Gospel is missing.

the level of the hermeneutics of the Scriptures, but emphasized the characteristics which might help the understanding of the essential significance of the study and often omitted the secondary problems. In the chapter on Pauline theology and the Fourth Gospel, he centered his explanation on their rôles in history comparing them with Greek thoughts, but said very little about the ecclesiastical or theological concepts. Here lies the source of dissatisfaction on the side of theologians.[1] It should be noted, however, that this is the very attitude of Hatano who dealt with the content of the New Testament religion, not simply as an object of a particular church theology but as that of philosophy of religion. For Hatano philosophy and theology should constitute the two factors which are to be amalgamated in the philosophy of religion.

In 1917 he became a professor of the study of religion[2] at the University of Kyôto and continued to teach there nearly twenty years. And this may be said the official turning-point in his scholastic theme. Hereafter his subject-matter became philosophy of religion all through his life. It was, however, only in 1925 that the first outcome of his study in this domain was presented to the eyes of the public. In the meantime he translated the *Critique of Practical Reason* of Kant into Japanese in collaboration with Wakichi Miyamoto in 1918. In 1920 he issued his first systematical writing in the philosophy of religion, *What is the Philosophy of Religion? Its basic Problems.* Next year his interest in Greek philosophy was embodied in a book, *The History of Religious Thoughts* of the West, Vol. I. Greece. But after that his

---

1) Later when the *Philosophy of Religion* was published, Seigo Yamaya called it a work of philosophy without direct relation to Christian studies. Hatano protested that his philosophy of religion is grounded in the New Testament and stands upon it. Carl Michalson comments about it, saying, "Some force is added to Hatano's claim when it is known that this interchange was first revealed by Professor Yamaya himself in his address at Hatano's burial." (Cf. C. Michalson's *Japanese Contributions to Christian Theology*, pp. 102–103).
2) Later in 1922 the University of Kyôto established a second professorship in the Christian religion in the section of the study of religion which was offered to Hatano. It was and still is the first and only professorship in the study of Christianity ever established in a state university of Japan.

activity in writing ceased for nearly fourteen years.  An article on *St. Paul* (1928) may be the only exception that appeared in the course of these years.  When Hatano went to Kyôto, he was surrounded by several brilliant collegues.  Among them were Kitaro Nishida (the author of *A Study of Good,* which was translated into English in 1960), Kenjiro Fujii, Sanjûro Tomonaga, Yasukazu Fukada and a little later they were joined by Hajime Tanabe (whose English article, *Memento mori* appeared in the *Philosophical Studies of Japan,* Vol. 1.) and Tetsuro Watsuji (the author of *A Climate,* also translated into English in 1962).  Hatano was, however, rather reserved in expressing his thought in any form of writing for several years.  And during those days the thought which later took the form of the trilogy in his philosophy of religion was fostered.  We find here Hatano who had first stepped up to the stage of philosophy reappearing as a man of philosophy of his own.

The first of the trilogy was written in 1935, three years before his retreat from the University of Kyôto and the last was issued in 1943 in the worst days of the Second World War.  When we place the beginning of his systematical work in the field of the philosophy of religion in the year 1917 when he was invited to the University of Kyôto, we find that Hatano spent almost 25 years in accomplishing the system of his philosophy.  One may well compare this with the years which were spent by Kant in preparing the three books of his critical  philosophy.

The development of Hatano's thought in those years may be roughly divided into three different periods.  The first covers the preparatory period of seven or eight years beginning with his professorship at the University of Kyôto in 1917.  The second is the succeeding ten years when he saw a light to his study and tried to lay down the principles of his future system.  The third begins with the publication of the *Philosophy of Religion* in 1935 which was followed by the *Introduction to the Philosophy of Religion* in 1940, to the year 1943 when his final work, *Time and Eternity,* was presented to the public.

As we have seen, Hatano first set up himself as a student of the history of philosophy wherein he tried to locate the significance of Christianity and again in the latter he sought for the most pure form of religious content. German Idealism which was prevalent in that period served as a background for his reasoning. The most compact outcome of his study in this period was: *What is the Philosophy of Religion? Its basic Problems* (1920) in which the influences of Kant and Schleiermacher were remarkable. He opens the argument with the problems of 19th century empiricism which was an antithesis to the traditional theistic philosophy of a particular religion. But in such a positivistic method religion is dealt with simply from the point of view of the history of religion and the meaning of religion as such is not seriously asked. Hatano points at its methodological weakness and affirms the necessity of the philosophy of religion. In the *Philosophical Dictionary* he defines *Shûkyô Gaku* (science of religion) and states as follows:

" The science of religion should also be grounded on historical study. And it is true that history of religion presupposes a certain value as its stipulation. But it does not deal with the value as such. So the science of religion should go beyond the history of religion and examine the content and validity of the value which is presupposed in the history of religion. This is the *raison d'être* of the philosophy of religion."[1]

Also in this book he took up the relationship of theology and philosophy of religion. Theology as a study of a particular religion aims at the synthesis of life and knowledge in this particular religion. Naturally historical theology is separated from systematic theology.

---

1) *Iwanami Tetsugakujiten* (Philosophical Dictionary), Iwanami Shoten, 1932, (8th rev. ed.) p. 451.

The latter is based upon a "particular content of life in a certain religion," but endeavors to attain its "conceptual, systematical apprehension." But once the question about the criteria of the universal validity of its truth is raised and is referred to the essence of religion in general, philosophy of religion is asked for. And it was the critical philosophy of Kant's that served him as the criteria in those days. He states in the lecture on the *Philosophy of Religion in Kant*:[1]

> "The philosophy of religion in its new and true sense is the self-consciousness based upon the self-assertion of the reason, namely, of the world of eternal truth."

After the book was published, however, Hatano seems to have gone into a far deeper domain of religious study. At the same time, the new current of thoughts which had come from Germany after the First World War compelled him to reexamine his cherished standpoint based upon German Idealism and the critical philosophy of Kant. There was a sign of doubt in him that the Kantian philosophy which had directed the mind of young Hatano now appeared not very satisfactory as a real solution to the basic problems in the field of religion. The most influential thoughts which had taken over the Neo-Kantian philosophy and Husserl's phenomenology were the existential philosophy of Martin Heidegger and the critical theology of Barth and Brunner. After several years of extensive study of these thinkers, Hatano had to admit that although they had cultivated a new field of problems in philosophy and theology, they failed in bringing any basic, real solutions to the issues. The more vigorously were their arguments carried on, the further the discussion on the content of the truths of religious experience as such appeared to be pushed back. There was no other way for him than to rely on his own standpoint and method in discovering the reality of the "subject of religious experience." He started from the "really existing God"

1) See the Appendix I of *What is Philosophy of Religion? Its basic Problems.*

and the "God of Power," seeking for the "God of Truth" and finally reached the notion of the "God of Love". They were compiled in a book, *Philosophy of Religion,* in 1935. We should say that it was his colossal spiritual power that led him out of the tangles of an intellectual search in which he had been involved for more than ten years.

After he succeeded in publishing this book, he felt some need of paraphrasing his point of view and methodology, because in the book he had centered his mind entirely in essential issues without making many detailed explanatory remarks. In those days, however, the condition of his health was very unstable. In the early summer of 1937, just before his retreat from the University of Kyôto he suffered from stomach ulcer which lasted nearly a year. The next year his wife became sick and passed away in January, 1939. It was in this series of misfortunes that Hatano carried out the writing of the *Introduction to the Philosophy of Religion,* which appeared in 1940, a year before the outbreak of the Pacific War. Next year he moved from Kyôto to Tokyo where he lived with his adopted son's family, but after the War started in December, considerable difficulties, both financial and moral, caused by the abnormal situation of the time seem to have disturbed him in every respect. In spite of all the inconveniences and instability of the circumstances, he continued his writing for another two and half years. *Time and Eternity* appeared to the world in the very midst of the infernal days of the War in 1943.

Shortly after this book was published, the whole situation in Japan became more critical. And Hatano was obliged to evacuate from Tokyo to the north-eastern part of Japan in Iwate Prefecture. It is reported that in those days of refuge and hunger Hatano could find ample spiritual consolation in the reading of Plato's *Laws,* Dante's *Divine Comedy* and the Bible.

In April, 1947, two years after the end of the War, he returned to Tokyo to teach at Tamagawa Gakuen University by the friendly invitation extended by Mr. Kuniyoshi Obara. After that physically he became weaker than ever. It is said that he could not give his lectures very regularly. In 1948 he again suffered from cancer and had two operations, in August and September. Thereafter he was obliged to stay in bed most of the time. It was on the 17th of January, 1950 that he finally closed his 73 years' scholarly career.

As regards the structure of Hatano's philosophy of religion, there is a very thorough exposition by Professor Masanao Katayama in a book commemorating Dr. Hatano which was published in 1954.[1] It gives us a very precise and clear-cut picture of Hatano's basic points of view, such as his analysis of life in three stages of temporality, his understanding of idealism, and the notions of personalism and God which are developed in his conception of time and eternity. There is also a voluminous commentary on *Hatano's Philosophy of Religion* written by Dr. Yosuke Hamada.[2] Unfortunately these books are written in Japanese and inaccessible to Western readers. The only commentary on Hatano ever written in English may be that of Dr. Carl Michalson in the fourth chapter of his *Japanese Contributions to Christian Theology* (1960), which is dedicated to the evaluation of Hatano's philosophy, especially of his latest work, *Time and Eternity*. This is a unique and most excellent introduction to Hatano's philosophy of religion to the English-speaking public.

It may be of some use for the readers to give a general outline of Hatano's tripartite scheme which is developed in his *Time and Eternity*. As was mentioned above, Hatano started from the Kantian conception of " person " which led him to the analysis of

---

1) Ken Ishiwara, M. Katayama, K. Matsumura and M. Tanaka, *That which lies in the Basis of Religion and Philosophy...The Achievement of Dr. Seiichi Hatano*, Tokyo, Iwanami Publishing House, 1954.
2) Yosuke Hamada, *Hatano's Philosophy of Religion*, Tamagawa University Press, Tokyo, 1949. Also the Philosophical Society of the University of Kyôto issued a special edition of *Tetsugaku Kenkyû* (Study of Philosophy) in 1951, commemorating Hatano.

"basic human experience." The living whole of human experience is called life. And according to his expression, life disclosed itself in time. As the dynamic flow of life is called "experience", so the variable aspect of time in relation to human experience is named "temporality." Unlike so-called calender time or objective time, temporality is the time man experiences. And the time of human experience, for Hatano, is characterized by the type of love in which he lives. Accordingly, similar to the pattern of Schleiermacher's three levels of the relationship between the self and an other, Hatano establishes a tripartite scheme of natural, cultural and religious temporalities and tries to locate the kind of love which rules at each level of life.

The first stage of temporality is found in natural life, where the self goes into a direct relationship with others. It is characterized by desire (*epithumia*). At this stage, the present which forms the true existence or selfhood is kept in flux and always drained into its vacuum or nothingness of the past. But the future which is "about to come" (*shôrai* in Japanese, not *mirai, i.e.* future in the negative sense of not-yet-come-ness) replaces the present which is drifting into the non-beingness of the past. After some analysis of Augustine's psychological exposition of time and Bergsonian distinction of the experienced time from the technological (objective in Hatano) time, Hatano noticed that neither of them have really comprehended the future as the mediator (the supplier of being) between past (non-being) and present (being).[1] In the time of natural life, one enjoys himself by making others his object or his property. And by asserting himself against other, he not only averts their threat to him, but also tries to devour them in order to ascertain his own being or presentness. Thus the immediacy of the relationship between the selfhood and otherness is destroyed at the second stage of temporality.

1) Hatano, *Time and Eternity*, Eng. tr. p. 9

Cultural temporality is characterized by *erôs* where past and future are sucked up by the present which rushes along the road of self-realization. In cultural life others are absorbed into the orbit of a man's own self-realization.

> "In *erôs* the subject will expand into infinity, so that finally all existence in the world will be involved in the self, and the outwardness, the basic spatiality between the self and others, is seemingly overcome."[1]

Thus in cultural life, others lose the status of concrete reality which they once possessed in the immediacy of natural life. Quite contrary to natural time which is marked by its irreversibility, cultural time is reversible. The perishing present of natural time is superseded by "permanent presentness" (*nunc permanens*). Everything including past and future is possessed by the imperishable presentness of *erôs*.[2] As a result, the temporal aspect of cultural life is always expressed simply in its presentness. The past and future constitute only the inner structure of the present as contents of recollection and imagination. Cultural life prides itself on its character of this "permanent now" which is taken for a kind of conquering of temporality. It is, however, simply one homogeneous continuity of presentness. It is characterized by beginninglessness and endlessness, which are often mistaken as being analogous to eternity. Hatano agrees with Hegel in calling this endlessness or limitlessness "bad infinity" or "false infinity" which is nothing other than an incomplete, fragmentary and instable duration.[3] But so long as cultural time is life, it is obliged to face the end of its very existence. The end of its existence is called death. Death cuts off the relation between the self and others, *i.e.* between present and future. It is a complete negation of the existence of the self which stands all by itself. According to Michalson's phras-

---

1) Hatano, *Time and Eternity*, Eng. tr. p. 106
2) Hatano, *Philosophy of Religion*, p. 47.
3) Hatano, *Time and Eternity*, Eng. tr. pp. 54—55.

ing, "Hatano knows of only two kinds of answers to the tragedy of death: 1) by overcoming time in death, as in the Buddhist negation (deliverance) of the self, or 2) by overcoming death in time, as in the Christian conception of the fellowship of the self with the trustworthy otherness of God which, according to Hatano's phrase, is the 'time of love' or 'eternity'".[1]

When we think of the fact that *Time and Eternity* appeared in an epoch when the whole earth was thrown into a chaotic war of hatred and destruction, we are much impressed by the evidence of this muscular intellectual and spiritual capacity of Hatano's which gave birth to this positive answer of the time of love coming from the Other, or Eternity.

Carl Michalson comments on the status of Hatano in the future development of Christian thought in Japan:[2]

> Some feel a Hatano renaissance is imminent. "There will come a time," Professor Yamaya has said, "when to read the complete work of Hatano...will be the first duty of the Japanese theologian.[3] Others believe Hatano can have no serious impact upon contemporary Japan because he did not significantly take into account the more vital spirit of such currently influential figures as Kierkegaard, Dostoevsky, and Barth. He was critical of Heidegger and Barth, whereas the present generation prefers Heidegger and Barth and identifies Hatano with an earlier generation..." Hatano's personality and his style do seem to typify the pre-war mode. His insight, however, even in the setting of current Japanese thinking, is advanced. One would not realize this who had not struggled with his latest work, *Time and Eternity*. There it can be seen how classical, Biblical, and ex-

---

1) Michalson, *Japanese Contributions to Christian Theology*, p. 113.
2) Michalson, JCCT, p. 104.
3) Seigo Yamaya, *Modern Japan and Christianity* (Kindai Nippon to Kirisutokyô), Tokyo, 1956, p. 297.

istential categories come together in a study of time and being. This theme is in the forefront of current theological and philosophical discussion, and what Hatano contributes to its development merits a hearing.

To the end, we should like to add a word of gratitude to Professor Yosuke Hamada of Dôshisha University for the valuable manuscript on Hatano's thought which helped us a great deal in completing this preface. Also we owe a considerable part of this description on Hatano's life and his academic achievement to the article of Dr. Ken Ishiwara in " *That Which lies in the Basis of Religion and Philosophy* ". As to the comments on *Time and Eternity* we took the liberty of borrowing some passages from the very clear-cut analysis of Dr. Carl Michalson of Drew University.

THE EDITORIAL BOARD

# Preface

The problem of time and eternity has been the major concern of philosophy and religion throughout the ages. It is, in fact, one of the most difficult problems. In this book I have tried further to expand and develop the thoughts which I once propounded in my *Philosophy of Religion* some years ago. I must admit that some passages have resulted in sheer modification. It has long been my belief that this problem may only be solved by the close collaboration of philosophy and religion in mutual respect and understanding. Both are often used or drawn upon for the sake of evident expediency or approached in blind obedience which curries philosophical favor. Such attitudes or approaches, however, should be strictly avoided, for they injure the dignity and spoil the purity of the matter in question. Since this book stands within the discipline of philosophy, it is written as philosophy of religion.

As to the terms which are used in this book, I have followed the customary usage of today's academic circle and have tried as far as possible to avoid esoteric terminology. I have necessarily made one exception. This has to do with the words *shôrai* (future; literally, about-to-come-ness) and *mirai* (future; literally, not-yet-come-ness). In most cases in ordinary speech these words are used as synonyms. Academic people, however, probably from the habit of a long tradition, seem to have a special fondness for *mirai*. It is used even when it refers to such positive notions as " planning" or " expectation." This is a matter that needs to be reconsidered more carefully. I shall leave its detailed discussion to the main part of this book (pp. 2 & 148 seq.). In a few cases the two words are not necessarily identical in substance. Even if they were identical in most cases, it would be preferable to use *shôrai* which simply and positively expresses the basic *about-to-*

*come-ness* or imminence of things.  When that which is *about to come* has *not yet come,* it is called *mirai.*  *Mirai* should be considered, therefore, as a derivative phenomenon.  In its verbal form, *shôrai* can be expressed simply by conjugation, whereas in the case of *mirai* an adverb, not yet, needs to be added.  In this book, therefore, I have in every case adopted *shôrai* as a general term for expressing the future.

Author

January 1943

# Chapter One

# Natural Temporality

## ( 1 )

As " eternity " is interpreted in one way or another as something which transcends or surpasses time or temporality, the problem of " time and eternity " is also treated in many different ways depending on what the respective points of view are. Here we are going to deal with it from the standpoint of philosophy of religion. This study has already been stimulated by the heavy pressure of historical tradition since the time of Plotinus. As is explained later, it attracted our attention chiefly because of the fact that in religion the idea of " eternity " is revealed most clearly in its proper power, depth and maturity. " Eternity " is a concept which has been born essentially in religion. This fact will certainly illuminate the inquiry into " time " or " temporality ". Eternity, which is simply the content of our imagination, or which, as an objective reality, constitutes a mere object of theoretical cognition, is almost entirely meaningless in religion. Hence, as we take up the problem of time or temporality, we must pay special attention to its particular connotation. This can be easily anticipated from the close relationship between time and eternity. That is, we must step into the realm of our experience as such and grasp the true image of " the time " in which we are and in which we live. In other words, we must face the bare reality of the temporality of human life.

Already in our daily life we imagine and grasp time as a kind of order which governs all things, being and action in the world. And we think that by participating in it we obtain a measure and

1

law of cognition, common to all men. This is not the fundamental aspect of time at all, however. It is nothing but an objectified image of what we are living in, set before us and projected on the outer world. It is a secondary image which has been considerably transfigured by reflection. Those who wish to see the fundamental aspect of time should put aside entirely this kind of image for the moment and step into the depth of basic human experience. Of course, as experience is obliged to be apprehended by means of reflection, the image of objective time which is its very product tends to hinder our observation, hiding the object from our eyes and making our task very difficult, as St. Augustine once deplored.[1] Nevertheless to describe the reality of time in relation to our experience is the most essential and cardinal question to be asked.

( 2 )

We or our " selves " (shutai, subjects; literally: master-body or upholder of experience) live in the " present ". To the subjects who actually live or exist in the present, the " present " is synonymous with true being. Then, is experienced time or the fundamental phase of time simply exhausted in the present? As is often manifested in common-sense views as well as in those of the scholars, when one considers the present as a point which lacks either continuity or internal structure, this will be the inevitable conclusion at which one must arrive. In so far as a point signifies nothing but a sheer limit of some other existing being, and at the same time the future (shôrai) and the past (kako) which are to be limited by the present are actually non-existent, time in its essence should be reduced to a perfect void (kyo-mu; literally, void-nothingness).[2] This is, however, simply a wrong conclusion derived from a false attitude which, ignoring the time of

---

1) Augustine, *Confessions*, XI, 14.
2) Aristotle, *Physics*, 217b seqq., where this difficulty is already stated.

2

experience, merely tries to deal with objective time. As will be shown later, in the case of objective time it is inevitable to represent time after the analogy of space. Consequently, it is also permissible to represent the present as a point, or rather to do so is unavoidable, if time be treated as a mathematical quantity. Nevertheless, for those who wish to attain a true understanding of time it is absolutely necessary to break the yoke of such an image at the outset.

The present is not equivalent to a simple point. It has a certain extension and inner structure of its own.[1] It may be said, on the one hand, that in the realm of experience time resides in the present, but on the other hand, this present involves the past and the future as inevitable factors. Ceaselessly the present comes into being and ceaselessly it passes away. It comes into being from the "future" (*shôrai*) and passes away into the "past" (*kako*; literally: *pass-away*). When that which is about to come will come or will achieve being, it is the present. But as soon as the present comes into being, it passes away into non-being. This incessant flux or transience is called time. Thus both the future and the past are immanent in the present as the factors which make for its flow and transience. Here growing ever means perishing and coming into being always means passing away. To move and to live are the fundamental characteristics of the present and, accordingly, of time. So far as time exists, the flux continues and accordingly the present remains always present. But one should not presume from this that time as such is something like an unchanging order or law and that it is simply its content that changes or moves. As a fulfillment of the life of a subject or as an owner of its being, the present can never be found by itself, in separation from its content. Rather it is a being filled with its content. The present flows incessantly with its content and ever renews itself.

---

1) Augustine, *Confessions*, XI, 14 seqq. Generally speaking, the treatise on time in St. Augustine is an epoch-making work which even those who have a different point of view should esteem very highly.

If the future (*shôrai*) lies in the anticipation of what is *about to come* and the past lies in the sending off of what is *going away,* where does the future come from and where does the past go? In so far as the scope of our experience is strictly limited to the field of our experience, it seems that the answer should be equally to or from nothingness (*mu*) or " non-being." Perhaps there may not be much objection to considering the future as non-being, since it has *not yet come* (*mirai*). On the other hand, a strong opposition will be raised to identifying the past, that is, that which has been, with mere transition into non-being. In the first place, one may refute its non-beingness on the ground that the past will exist in or affect our consciousness as content of our recollection or memory. But as it will become clear, what is placed before the subject as content of recollection is actually that which has been objectified by reflection. So the mode of its being is not of the past, but of the present. The recollection is an act of a subject living at present. Its content is the objects placed before this subject. Then one may raise the next question. What is experienced should be, in some way or other, a being. And in as much as " nothingness " or " non-being " cannot be experienced as such, the transition into non-being should also transcend our experience. If so, would the past, experienced as a factor belonging to the inner structure of time, be nothing other than sheer imagination? If the same logic can be applied to the future, would it be only the present which remains so far as we talk about the time of experience...? To this objection we answer that the fact that nothingness or non-being cannot be experienced *as such* does not mean that it can never be experienced at all *in any way.* The nothingness or non-being as such which is separated from being is actually a content of meaning objectified by our reflection. As such it is rather a being or an entity. The act of simply apprehending non-being as such can be accomplished rather in its beingness or presentness.[1] Nevertheless,

---

1) It is the merit of Plato's *Sophist* that this point was made clear for the first time.

it is not rejected as a logical contradiction or paradox, but can be an object of our thinking and understanding as meaningful content. It is owing to the fact that non-being is based upon and springs from our experience. In this case, too, our experience has the power of resolving any logical doubt. Nothingness can be experienced in and through such experiences of want, emptiness and perishing which require it as their medium. The same can be said of the experience of time. As soon as the present comes from the future (*shôrai*), it perishes into non-being. Thus the experience of nothingness (*mu*) is simply that of the disappearance of being or of what has existed, in other words, the experience of the past at present. That is to say, time is the most fundamental characteristic of the being of life. Through the experience of time we can get deepest living experience, thinking and apprehension of nothingness (*mu*). In dealing with the experience of falling into non-being by means of reflection, we can proceed into the thinking and understanding of nothingness as such.

When we, from the clear indications of our experience, frankly acknowledge the fact that the past means perishing or falling into non-being and that what has become past is non-existent, we attain the most important first step which has fundamental significance on the way to the solution of the problem of " time and eternity ". The next step of similar importance is the correct understanding of the " future " (*shôrai*). Temporarily we have already adopted with reservation the view that the essence of the experience of the future (*shôrai*) lies in the expectation (welcoming) of what is about to come from non-being, and that so far as it is distinguished from the present, we consider the future as non-being. Seeing that the future is renamed in Japanese as *mirai* (not-yet-come), a nomination which already implies its non-beingness, we can say that this is the most current and rather natural interpretation. But a closer observation will disclose that this interpretation is wrong. If we pay attention to what experience tells us, we must say that what a subject expects in time, that is, in the medium of the "future" (*shôrai,* about-to-come) in the present, is neither nothingness (*mu*) nor non-being, nor being coming from non-being, but simply being. New being (present) replaces the being (present) which has vanished into non-being. The act of anticipating (welcoming) being does not contradict the basic inclination of self-assertion (*i. e.* self-preservation and self-expansion) of the subject. It is rather the most natural expression of this inclination. So far we must say that it is an experience of joy where we cannot find any factor of nothingness (*mu*). Therefore, in order to understand the fundamental nature of future, it is not quite adequate to substitute the word *mirai* (future or *not-yet-come-ness*) for *shôrai* (future or *about-to-come-ness*). It is only when its meaning is interpreted in relation to the past that *shôrai* can become *mirai*. That is, "*mirai*" is a derivative concept in contrast to "*shôrai*". *Shôrai* can be a *mirai* and what comes can come from nothingness (*mu*), because the present, *i.e.* being, constantly flows away and never remains as present. The present toward which something is headed is different from the present at which something is arriving. What is heading toward *a* "now" must arrive at another "now". In other words, it is because of the past that the present can never meet the future (*shôrai*) which is coming toward it. The factor of nothingness which changes *shôrai* into *mirai* is not inherent in *shôrai* itself but is furnished by the past. In short, *shôrai* simply becomes *mirai* so far as it has the office of refilling the gap of the perishing present and the disappearing being which was created by the past. Therefore, *shôrai* is not necessarily a *mirai*. If an imperishable present or endless now—*i.e.* eternity—will reveal itself, it is the past that will disappear first, but also the *mirai* should follow the same destiny as the past. As it is more clearly stated later, however, *shôrai* will not only continue to exist as the sustainer of the present, but will also gain its newly brilliant significance as a source of an imperishable being.[1]

( 3 )

In order to make the above-mentioned points more comprehensible, and to clarify the true aspect of time in further detail, let us examine ontologically its significance for the existence of the self. We shall then discover the fact that at the level of the actual life, that is, the natural and cultural life the basic structure of the subject is time. Temporality is the most essential characteristic of human nature. The existence of the subject is directed toward others.[2] It gains and maintains itself in the relationship and contact with others. On the other hand, it is the natural life which constitutes the foundation of all being. In ancient Greece the word nature (φύσις) was used to signify a being, most basic and fundamental, in opposition to the notion of whatever is artificial and man-made. Such ideas as being as such, simplicity, or immediateness are attributed to it. At the level which we call natural life, the existing subject stands in an immediate contact and relationship with the existing others. To live in this way is the most basic and fundamental aspect of human life. Cultural, human life is built on this basis. It is true that as our life reaches higher stages its temporality will also be somewhat transformed, but what determines its essential mode of being is natural life. Hence it will be understood how temporality stretches its roots into the base

---

1) It is almost a commonplace in academic circles in Japan rather carelessly to call *shôrai mirai.* This is not an adequate usage of the words. We should reconsider or rather cease to mix them up. Even when they are used as identical in substance, the former is a positive expression simply seen from the front, and the latter is the product of a derivative attitude which tries to see the implication of events from behind. Verbally speaking, *shôrai* is expressed simply in the form of a grammatical future which is represented in such phrases as *"Kitaran"* (may-come) or *"Kitaraba"* (if-come), whereas we must add an adverb in order to express *"mirai"* (not-yet-come). The same thing can be observed in τὸ μέλλον or ὁ μέλλων (sc. χρόνος) in Greek and *futurum* in Latin as well as in other modern languages.

2) In this regard see my *Philosophy of Religion* and *Introduction to Philosophy of Religion.* Also see § VII, 1.

of human nature and how firmly and almost fatally it colors the nature of our life.

The subject insistently asserts its being as reality. In other words, it tries to maintain or even to enlarge its being over against others. This is its essential tendency. And it is the tendency of natural life in general. As a *locus* of fellowship in the immediacy of existence it manifests the following two characteristics. The subject would be dispersed in air and reduced to ashes if there were no others to come into contact with it. That is, it maintains its existence only through other real beings which intrude, resist, cause tension in it and thus drive it to self-assertion. Moreover, the content of the life of the subject is constituted only as symbols which signify and represent others in this real fellowship. Accordingly the existing others should be considered as those which maintain and supply for the subject the contents of reality and livelihood as well as of all being. On the other hand, as natural life is a direct and, therefore, superficial contact or encounter between real existences, for the subject it is a pressure or invasion of others and a loss of being. So long as one lives the natural life, the subject is gaining as well as losing its being. Here to become is to perish and to come is to go away.

In this incessant flux of natural life we shall find the most fundamental aspect of time and temporality, that is, natural time or natural temporality. In the center stands the " present ", where the life is accomplished and to which its existence belongs through the self-assertiveness of the subject. It embraces within itself the entirety of time. The " past ", on the other hand, is a destruction of life, a privation of existence, and a draining off into non-being. And it is the " future " which serves as a mediating agency between the subject and others. Since it supplies existence to the present which is ever flowing away or to the being which is ever perishing, the future plays the rôle of maintaining the present. But at the same time it becomes the cause of the present's ceaseless transition into the past. What is about to come (*shôrai*) becomes the present when it comes, but at the same time, it never encounters the present which it attempts to reach. This contradiction which is found between the future and the present indicates that the subject and others do not share the real fellowship of life and existence. As will be stated later, here we shall find the main clue for solving temporality at the level of eternity.

Our point of view will be strengthened by a short historical survey. St. Augustine's treatise on "Time" is an epoch-making work from which anyone who tries to deal with this theme should begin and should consult as his guide.[1] By admitting that the reality of time lies in the "present" which has a duration furnished with a certain inner structure, he disclosed the true aspect of time in the depth of our experience. Time is called by him the extension of mind (*distentio animi*). That is, the present is not something simple and undifferentiated, but involves the future and the past in it. According to him, the present consists of three modes or moments linked together. As time is the basic *modus essendi* of the subject, to these three moments correspond three basic acts of the subject. That is to say, the present consists of intuition (*contuitus*); the future, of expectation (*expectatio*); the past, of memory (*memoria*) ... It is certainly the defect of this theory that Augustine did not think of the basic difference between natural time, which constitutes the foundation, and cultural time, which forms its super-structure. Of course, "expectation" can safely be included in it as corresponding to the future (*shôrai*) in natural time. But "memory" is, as will be discussed later, an act which belongs to the level of cultural, historical life. And when we think of the fact that cultural life is an attempt at liberating life from natural life, we may be able to understand that his conception of "time" meant nothing other than the *modus vivendi* of the subject which is put in absolute isolation. After all, he failed to realize the truth that future (*shôrai*) is an indication

1) *Confessions*, XI, 14, seqq.

of the mode of living of the human subject which maintains its existence in its relationship with existing others. He simply distinguished eternity from time, and failed to grasp it as a real conqueror of time in the dynamic relationship with it.

In the profound insight of Bergson's essay on *Time and Free Will* we must appreciate his intention of reducing time from sheer representation of a derivative or secondary value to its basic form given in the depth of our very experience. He tried to separate from fundamental experience all the activity of the subject which aims at a practical outcome, or in this sense at the future. If his interesting metaphysical point of view be put aside in this connection, it would certainly be justifiable that he gave secondary significance to cultural time. Likewise, without taking his metaphysics into consideration, we may appreciate in his philosophy the disclosure that time comes into being in the form of "duration". He maintained that in time the contents of thought are mixed and interrelated. And while distinguishing the time of experience from objective time, which is represented spatially, and putting an emphasis upon the basic characteristics of the former, he came to comprehend the time of experience as duration, which has an inner structure. But we must admit that he was entirely at fault in omitting the future (*shôrai*) from the time of basic human experience. As a result, his *durée* consists merely of the past and the present. In this case, contrary to the real order, the past precedes the present and therefore provides the present with its being. In other words, mingling with and permeating the present, the content of the past constructs a duration, or an all-inclusive present. The content of the past comes entirely from memory. Thus time as duration will be nothing but cultural time, without a future. What is the source of these errors? Of course, the cause lies in the fact that the subject is left in the solitude of isolation. There the subject which experiences duration, abandoning its attitude of devoting itself in life for the benefit of others, retreats to the level

10

of reflection where it tries to contemplate itself in the mirror of self-consciousness. The method of cognition called intuition is used to avoid abstract thinking. However, it has shifted to the level of reflection, away from that of fundamental experience.

## ( 4 )

From the essential structure of time and temporality explained above, we may be able to develop and grasp several formal characteristics of temporality which become even more important in the face of and in relationship to eternity.

The first point has to do with the direction of time. It may be said that time moves either out of the future into the past by way of the present or, on the contrary, out of the past into the future. This contradiction may have some significance, suggesting the problems latent in the conception of time,[1] but, as the later discussion will show, it can be solved only by distinguishing different stages of temporality. At the level of the natural time of experience, that is, in the most basic and proper aspect of temporality, the direction is headed from the future to the past. And this direction is absolutely irreversible. What has gone into the past is reduced to nothingness. It is simply and truly non-being. What is reduced to nothingness is something irretrievable, beyond the reach of the subject's disposition and therefore something absolute. The past can never be present. This is the original aspect of time. It is called the irreversibility (*Unumkehrbarkeit*) of time. In short, the most basic direction of time or the most essential characteristic of temporality is the direction from reality into nothingness, from being into non-being.

In the second place, temporality signifies instability and perishableness. Time and existence in time lie in an incessant flux and transience from being into nothingness, and, for lack of rest or reflection, they rush down the road of self-destruction.

---

1) Lotze, *Metaphysik*, II, 3.

In connection with this, temporality signifies fragmentariness and incompleteness. The temporal being is always perishing and thus falling into privation. In the present the subject possesses its own existence. But the possession will immediately turn into privation and existence cannot be secured in perpetuity. The essential characteristic of time is that it can never be perfect, never gain its own selfhood. It will always be fragmentary.

Fourthly, temporality as formed in the direct relationship between the subject and existing others signifies, on the one hand, headlong devotion and, on the other, a limitation imposed upon the self-assertiveness which forms the core of selfhood (*shutaisei, subjecticity*). This can never be solved by an arbitrary decision or an effort of the subject. It is a destiny which one cannot escape.

Lastly, where living means perishing, where to be signifies not to be, where the meaning of life is not realized, where everything ends in a dream and where the subject nevertheless can do nothing about this situation in his own power, the negation of the meaning of life, a want of happiness, a feeling of emptiness, uneasiness, sadness and disappointment will be the inevitable result. In so far as "eternity" is the overcoming of time, it should signify the entire elimination of these characteristics of life.

# Chapter Two

# Culture and Cultural Temporality

## 1. Culture

### ( 1 )

Cultural temporality springs from the soil or womb of natural temporality. In order to understand this, however, we must first observe the general foundation of culture and the cultural life.

The word culture (*bunka*) carries an implication of getting rid of the direct linkage with real, existing others or of liberation from the encounter with, the restriction from, or the tension within natural life. The subject is basically a being which has a center of independence by virtue of which it lives. Its essence, that is, its selfhood (*shutaisei*, subjecticity) lies in its reality and manifests itself in the form of self-assertion. When this real, existing subject meets or encounters equally existing others face to face and rushes on to its self-achievement and expansion, it cannot but end in annihilation of the others and at the same time of itself. The being of the subject is naturally directed toward others and apart from the liaison with others, there would be no selfhood. But if a being in the realm of natural life asserts itself against others to the finish, in contradiction of its primary motive, it will invite the destruction of its own being. The essence of cultural life lies in the overcoming of this difficulty as it liberates itself from the pressure and intervention of the others and completely asserts itself in the realm of freedom. Therefore, however primitive our actual life may be, however immature or inferior in grade, so long as it continues to exist, it contains in some degree or other a

13

certain form of culture. Natural life is the basis of the link of development which is not to be reached nor unmasked until the theoretical analysis traces it back to that stage. In fact, it can never exist all by itself.

The liberation and freedom of the subject in cultural life is attained by the formation of its "object" (*kyakutai*). It is true that the being of the subject ever directs itself to the other being, and its selfhood (*shutaisei*) is always manifested in its self-assertion. But now the real, existing being retreats from the seat of the other and the "object" takes its place. The object is a conceptual being rather than an actual one. Originally in natural life it formed the content of the life of the subject, symbolizing the real, existing other, but then, abandoning its rôle, it entered into a state of separation and retaining the trait of real otherness, was placed before the subject at a distance. Now the separation of the object, when conversely observed, is the separation of the subject. This separation or opposition of the subject and the object is called "reflection". By means of reflection, self-consciousness or awareness comes to the surface along with awareness of the object. Thus the subject as " I " or " Self " (*ego*) comes into being. At the level of natural life the subject was fully engaged in real, existing others and had no time for contemplating the others around him. Only at the level of culture where it secures ease and relaxation and enjoys freedom and independence, does it proceed to the assertion and realization of its own being. Now how can this be carried out? In order to understand this, that is, in order to understand the true meaning of culture, we must take a further step in the observation of the dual aspect or characteristic of the object.

( 2 )

Of course, the object as such does not simply belong to the subject nor simply form the content of our consciousness. But unlike real, existing being, the object as ideal being stands in a much closer position to the subject and barely maintains its semi-independence. Its being is directed to or against the subject. That is, contrary to the real, existing being which exists as an independent center and lives in and acts through it, the ideal (or conceptual) being has no such independent center. The subject, as real, existing being, persistently sticks to this hidden center and refuses to abandon itself to the possession of others; whereas the object as ideal being is a plain, disclosed being without any hidden center or depth. Its being does not obtain stability unless it is taken into the subject and becomes a part of the selfhood of the subject. To that extent it is a rootless being, floating in air. As a disclosed being, it is the object of contemplation. In short, the attitude of the subject toward the object should take the form of contemplation.

Secondly, the object is an ideal being, but at the same time, it is an "other" against which the subject asserts itself. But unlike the case of the subject facing directly toward real, existing others, it here develops itself in accordance with the mode of being of the object, and achieves itself not by eliminating the others, but by developing its hidden self in the very others. Self-realization is the very basic act of cultural life. From this one can say that the duty of the object is entirely fulfilled by disclosing its real self to the subject. That is, its otherness lies in its possible selfhood. Now the self-realization of the subject is an act of disclosing something hidden and of revealing itself from its real, existing center to a clearer fringe or surface of ideal being. This may be called "expression.". It is true that we owe to Leibnitz the ingenious insight that the essence of the cultural subject lies in its self-expression.[1] He extended it, however, to all existing being, that is, to all beings that have centers by virtue of which they act. Following tradition he called it "substance". As it becomes clear later, he simply elevated actual cogni-

---

1) Leibnitz employs the terms *exprimer* or *représenter*.

tion of the world of objective reality to the height of metaphysical doctrine.

Objects maintain their existence as others only as expressions of the subject. And this will create a similar relationship among objective beings. Of course, the contents of objects are alien to each other, but in so far as they are all expressions of the subject, they also express each other. So here appears a phenomenon peculiar to the world of objects. That is, objects as ideal beings stand in a relationship with a real existing subject and thus they acquire the character of " meanings ". The meanings are expressions of what is inner or hidden, but at the same time as they are governed or bound by a common center, they have certain commonness or linkage among themselves. This is the essential character of meanings. An entirely isolated object which is nothing but a point is, like the subject separated from others, only a product of abstraction or imagination. A meaningless object is the equivalent of darkness. It cannot carry out the duty of expression nor can it any longer be an object of contemplation. Thus objects acquire their meaning when they are supported by the subject which is the center of their beings. On the contrary, the subject will also be saved from being a sheer entity hidden in darkness by expressing itself in objects. So it is true that the subject stands in a hidden center and derives its life and action from it, but its existence is entirely exhausted in the being of objects, so far as it contains in it a disclosed, contemplated and interpreted being, that is, meaningful being. Every attempt to grasp the subject as such, independently of objects or objective relationships or the reference of meanings, should fail. Objects as expressions of the subject represent the latter from start to finish.

This can be said, however, in so far as objects would have fulfilled the duty of expression and the self of the subject has been actualized in it. But in reality this can never happen. Objects are expressions of the subject, but at the same time they stand against it in a position of otherness. So long as they are others, objects remain only as possible selves of the subject. They connote material in which the selfhood of the subject will be realized. But if they ever simply remain pure possibility, the selfhood will never become actualized and consequently objects also will lose their being. Therefore, in objects the characters of both form and actuality should be furnished. Thus it is a *sine qua non* for the formation of objects as well as for that of the cultural subject that the two series of concepts—selfhood, actuality and form on the one hand, and otherness, possibility and matter on the other—should always be present as their necessary, essential factors. Unilateral accomplishment of one of them may mean after all an end of all existence. For example, if only otherness be driven home, it will return to the real otherness and culture will be buried in the grave of natural life and its extermination of self. On the other hand, if selfhood alone be claimed, the subject will exhaust itself on the surface of others and lose both the others which had been the objects of activity and its own center which is the source of its activity and will disappear just like an empty dream or contentless hallucination. The loss of others will equally mean death to the subject.

( 3 )

To elucidate the true structure of cultural life which is based on this dual character of objects, let us distinguish " expression " from " symbol ". They are not always two contradictory ideas. Rather they are correlative. Expression can be effected by symbolization and symbol is an expression of something. We can also say that all expressions are symbols and, contrariwise, that all symbols are expressions.[1] Both can be called an expressing action (expression) or

---

1) Cassirer, *Philosophie der symbolischen Formen.* 3 Bde. This is an interesting and instructive essay which explains the whole sphere of culture by means of symbols.

indicating action (symbol). Each implies two moments of oneness and otherness and thus discloses the dual aspect of identity and difference. In putting special emphasis here on the factor of unity or identity in expressions and of otherness in symbols, we shall establish discrete fields of application for the two concepts, so that we may be able to see the points of difference and clarification.

(a)　Expression

As stated above, "expression" is held completely within the subject's scope of influence. It is the self of the disclosed subject, or, it is the disclosing act of this self, if we name it action. The otherness which is retained in it is only that of objects. Its essence is more or less in its possible selfhood. It is true that the subject still survives there in full force as a hidden center. But as long as it is a subject of expression, it expresses its self completely at the surface and in achieving its aim, erases its self. Even if it were to succeed in not destroying itself, it would be driven into unavoidable isolation. Of course, living in the domain of culture, the subject can never entirely cut the link with the existing reality of others. But culture as such does not essentially depend on any real others. Here the direct target of the subject is the objects which are placed in a state separated from the reality of others. Their duty is simply to disclose the self of the subject. This is true not only when the existing being which is the foundation of the object is a thing, but also when it is a person.[1] At the cultural level, the contents of life or the objective world common to the " I " and " other people " are built and maintained, but a relationship between really existing beings which is to be formed between " I " and " Thou ", that is, a personal relationship in its strict sense, is almost non-existent. Even though we take the position that there is no such being as a person except oneself, we must assume theoretically that culture can still be found there. The other

---

1)　As to the distinction of "person" and "thing", see my *Philosophy of Religion*, § 29 seqq.

people who appear in the realm of culture are only material objects through which the subject achieves or expresses itself. Seen in terms of the basic character of culture, other people are simply "matter" and nothing else. Thus immanence and solitude are the essential characteristics of expression or of the subject. The *Monadology* of Leibnitz may be the most clear and adequate exposition of this. In the realm of culture, the subject is considered by him to be a "windowless" monad. The same thing can be said of the theory of Hegel, who developed the notion of the subject into that of "absolute mind". After all, culture is an achievement or expression of the self. Consequently it is an intrinsic act of the subject which drives it into independence. Strictly speaking, one cannot find there any others, that is, any really existing others over against the subject. In general, when advocacy of culture takes the form of metaphysics, it tends to follow the way of pantheism. There the others which confront the absolute subject or god have no other significance than as materials for the realization of the self. And even though formation or creation out of nothing be taught, the "nothing" will simply mean matter having the characteristic of potential being.[1]

(b) Symbol

Unlike expression, "symbol" comes into being in relationship or fellowship with really existing others.[2] When the contents of the life of the subject are alienated into objects and obtain the meaning of the plain form of the subject, they are called expressions; whereas when the same contents are related to the center of a really existing being which transcends the realm of the subject, responsible for disclosing not the self but others, and indicating or representing a really existing other being, they are called symbols. Expressions are immanent in the subject, whereas symbols transcend the subject. Symbols take their place on a line connecting one center with another, standing

---

1) See p. 119 seq.
2) As to the notion of symbol, its difference from "expression" was once discussed in my *Philosophy of Religion* (see §§ 5, 26, 41, 44, 45, 47, 48 etc.), but in this book I have made much clearer distinction of the two.

between two entities which otherwise can never meet. Without symbol they are simply obliged to repel each other. A symbol furnishes a hinge for conjoining the two, so that in a certain sense the penetration of an other reality into the subject may become possible and thus the subject will be saved from the state of isolation or self-denial. Symbol reassures the being of the subject toward others. This is life's proper aspect. In so far as there is a center, there must be symbols. In so far as there are symbols, there must be a center. When symbols are gone and the subject hears no voice of others, nothing will be left for the subject but death. When life is lifted to the level of culture, symbols are the same as expressions, but expressions are not always the same as symbols. By performing its duty, expression forces the subject to disappear. On the other hand, symbol connects the subject more closely with others and fortifies the basis of its being. Expressions cannot save us from temporality, but thanks to symbols, we can ascend to the realm of eternity, as we shall later see.

## 2. Activity and Contemplation

### ( 1 )

Let us now enter into the main line of our discussion. As we have seen above, objectivity consists of a series of dual factors or aspects such as otherness and selfhood, possibility and actuality, matter and form. These are the inevitable factors for the determination of an object, and the fellowship and tension existing between these two comprise the very reality of cultural life. That is to say, everywhere in the field of objects one can observe both of these factors existing together, but as the object itself as well as its two constituent elements are all expressions of the self, the two elements are disclosed as objects which are separated from or opposed to each other. Thus for the sake of the self-realization of the subject, it is necessary that the world of objects consist of two phases or realms, each of which has its dominant factor. The self-realization of the subject is carried out as an interaction of these two domains of objects. In other words, as it is stated above, although the objects are the expressions of the subject, yet the self can only be disclosed in reference to the content of objects. Apart from the mutual linkage of objects, the selfness of the subject is not apprehended. For example, if the linkage disappears and simply the content remains, the two factors may disappear at the same time. Moreover, it may mean a general disappearance of objects as a whole as well as of the subject itself. Since selfhood and otherness are the two distinguishing features of objects, they both should maintain their existence as objects, so that the connotations of the two should be expressed as different objective contents, separated one from the other, yet at the same time correlated. In other words, in the determination of the objective world, the two opposing factors which comprise the content of objects will also stand in mutual relationship. And yet the link should retain the two factors in itself in the respect that it retains the objective beings in it. That is, as their contents are related to each other in so far as they bear their respective meanings and responsibilities of selfhood and otherness, they are obliged to be separated and opposed to each other. In and through such relationship the self will achieve itself. One can put this simply in the following manner. That which stands before the object and asserts itself in it is the subject which exists from a hidden center. The subject realizes itself by acting upon objects. Moreover, in order that this self-realization may take the form of a cultural act, the subject should be disclosed as such. In other words, it acts upon an object only when it changes itself into one. Therefore, it realizes itself in a relationship of two objects which have different contents and meanings respectively, the one in the place of selfhood, the other in the place of otherness. And in so far as cultural life is built upon this relationship, it manifests the characteristic of "activity". This is the most basic and essential feature of the cultural life.

Here we notice how culture is built upon the basis of natural life and how cultural temporality is influenced by the natural temporality upon which it stands. What introduces the feature of activity into cultural life is the coexistence and correlation of the two factors of selfhood and otherness. In this case, otherness makes this activity possible as potentiality and matter, but, on the other hand, it hinders the self-realization which is the essence of this activity. The subject is able to actualize itself in the object owing to its otherness. But at the same time, so long as the object is an other, it is opposed to the subject and, retaining some distance from it, forces the subject to remain in its undisclosed selfhood. The other makes the subject the center of relationship or fellowship with it and gives it the character of a self, but, on the other hand, it leaves this self something undisclosed, impotent and therefore non-existent. The object is, however, a symbol of the other which is transferred into the expression of the self. So after all its otherness is simply a lingering taste of the original source. The source of this otherness should be sought for in the really existing otherness. We have already talked about the dual character of otherness in natural life.[1] On the one hand, the other and hence the future plays the rôle of making possible the subject's present and of supplying its existence; but on the other hand the future induces the present or existence into the non-existence of the past. As a result, time manifests itself as incessant flux and existence always remains in a state of incompleteness, fragmentariness and meaninglessness. In correspondence with this, at the level of cultural life, while the two factors of selfhood and otherness are anticipating and stimulating each other, they are, at the same time, resisting and excluding each other. Thus cultural activity, while it is moving toward a goal of realization, nevertheless must seek a destination which moves constantly beyond the horizon. Continuation without limit and tension without security are the destiny which culture must inevitably undergo.

---

1) See p. 7 seq.

(2)

We have already mentioned that the attitude of the subject toward the object lies in contemplation. But now it becomes clear that the basic characteristic of culture inheres in its activity. Are not these two propositions mutually exclusive? Contemplation and activity — θεωρία and πρᾶξις — are standards which represent two distinct camps in philosophy that have opposed each other ever since the time of ancient Greece.[1] Will there be any compromise of the two? If so, where will the link lie? We can answer this in the following manner. In so far as activity is the general characteristic of cultural behavior, contemplation should also be regarded as a kind of activity. Only it is an activity which has a special meaning and particular destination. That is, its goal or aim is to deepen its own proper meaning by getting rid of or overcoming the characteristic of activity, despite the fact that it is itself an activity. This can be achieved by mitigating or resolving the tension between the two factors within the content of the object. We have observed that the two factors of selfhood and otherness are represented in two kinds of expressions. What is proper to activity in particular is that the objective world is divided into two aspects or fields each representing respective factors, establishing between them a relationship of that which acts with that which is acted upon. As this tension is mitigated, form will approach actuality, the self will express itself more clearly and, at the same time, possibility will be lessened and the hidden being be disclosed. So far as the object as such keeps its distance from the subject, both aspects, each of which contains its own content, will perdure, but the tension which prevails between these heterogeneous contents will be released and the subject will cease to act and will remain quiet, contemplating

1)  Cf. Franz Boll, *Vita Contemplativa*, 1922; Werner Jaeger, *Ueber Ursprung und Kreislauf des philosophischen Lebensideals*, 1928.

the clear, transparent image of the objects. The subject will completely express itself, hide itself in the back-ground of the objects and will not disclose itself clearly in a position of the object and simply remain hidden as a center of the object's being. That is, it will retreat from the stage of life. Contrary to activity where, as the active self is disclosed, life is tinged with subjective color, life in contemplation is characterized by its objectivity. The essential trend of contemplation, however, does not admit of repose, either. So long as the object is opposed by some distance to the subject, otherness as well as selfness will still remain even though they may be simply immanent factors that constitute each content. If so, does this not mean that the active nature has not been completely overcome? In as much as a certain content remains as an object, it can never be a simple being. It contains within it the double factor which reveals the link of the unity and differences.

Again, one may put it this way. There are three kinds of otherness.[1] The first is the otherness of an existing reality toward another existence; the second is the otherness of an object toward a subject (existing reality) ; the third is the otherness between objects. The development of natural life into cultural life signifies deliverance from the first category of the otherness of existing realities, but it means, at the same time, a creation of the second and third kinds of otherness. Between the last two, the second, that is, the otherness of objects, is of more basic importance. The otherness which is the essence of objectivity creates a relationship between the one and the other in the very contents of the objects. Now the selfhood which is opposed to objectivity is a hidden, existing center. This center discloses itself in the objective otherness as it employs the latter as its material. Thus the object will take on the dual aspects or factors of selfhood and otherness. But estrangement between the two does not cease at this level. That is, the two are not only the constituent factors immanent

---

1) Concerning these three forms of otherness, see several passages of my *Philosophy of Religion*, especially § 44.

in the object, but rather, because of that, they should uncover or disclose themselves as two distinct fields of selfhood and otherness. Allegorically speaking, selfhood and otherness constitute dual layers of the object which is first formed by reflection. But so far as the two layers are separated, however thin the phase of the object may look, in reality it has some thickness, depth and profundity. If it remain as such, the layer which lies in the background (selfhood) may be obliged to maintain its completely concealed being. Therefore, the necessary second step toward the formation of an object will be that this submerged layer come to the surface. Thus both of the dual factors which are immanent in its content should come to the surface and manifest themselves as two distinct domains in the phase of objects, and that otherness should become a link between the contents of the objects. Because of the existence of the two layers of the foreground and background and of their tension, and consequently, on account of the struggle of the background to come to the fore, the surface of objects cannot be calm, nor smooth nor plane. It cannot help but see deviation or bring in instability. This is called activity. Now, the ultimate end of contemplation lies in smoothing the unevenness of the object and reducing it to a perfect plane. But can that possibly be done? And if so, how? Even though an object is something that is to be contemplated or to be disclosed, so long as it is set before the subject, it can never be purely even. Therefore, the subject which once tried to deliver itself from the nature of activity, should proceed further in the deliverance from all otherness. That is to say, by expressing itself completely and disclosing itself without reservation, the subject will totally merge with the object and, on the other hand, the object will cease to be an other and be reduced to the possession of the subject and be ended by the perfect unity of the two. And in order to achieve this, for the contemplation which rests on the hypothesis of the distance (however small it may be) of the subject and object, there is no other way than to abandon itself by thoroughgoing self-realization. Since ancient times, mysticism has tried to attain such a state of mind and believed in its possibility.[1] Unfortunately the success would be tantamount to reducing everything to dream or vanity. The subject without others has no other course than to die.

All this teaches us that contemplation cannot be the highest form of life, and therefore cultural life should be surpassed or superceded by a much higher stage of life.[2] But without going into detail, and restricting our observations to cultural life, we shall try to achieve an understanding of temporality. We saw that the essence of cultural life lies in its activity. But so long as it acts, the subject persistently asserts and discloses itself and at the same time it is reluctant to cut the link with others. This is the connection with temporality. In other words, so long as the real subject does not give up its original inclination of self-assertion, temporality, which is the fundamental structure of the subject, also constitutes the basic structure of cultural activity. But as the others here signify objects, the meaning of temporality is somewhat transformed. The embodiment of cultural life seen from the phase of temporality is "history". Therefore one finds cultural time only as historical time. Of course, we employ the term "history" here in its widest sense. How the inner structure of history thus interpreted looks in detail is a question unrelated to our present purpose and we must exclude it from our consideration. Likewise, the standpoint of temporality, it does not matter whether the subject be individual or collective.

( 3 )

Before going into the details of historical temporality, we shall expand our view of the act of contemplation and its special features. Contemplation is an act of freeing itself from activity notwithstanding

---

1) Concerning mysticism, see my *Philosophy of Religion*, § 21 seqq., § 45.
2) See my *Philosophy of Religion*, § 26 seqq., § 37 seqq.

the fact that it *is* a kind of activity. And this fact will lead us to modify the notion of temporality. Contemplation is roughly divided into "aesthetic contemplation", or appreciation, and "cognition". In aesthetic contemplation the object is free and isolated from natural reality, but no positive attitude is openly taken to remain in this isolated state. Although its content has no intention of symbolizing really other being, it still remains in the concreteness of natural life. On the other hand, in cognition, estranged conceptual beings obtain their stability and maintain their independence and transcendence. That is, the objects are stabilized. Thus their contents become more abstract and universal. The distance from natural life becomes more remarkable and the deliverance from it becomes more evident. As we have seen, once the subject achieves its end in contemplation, it expresses itself fully and entirely disappears into the background of objects. As a result, its temporality may have to be overcome. This will be explained later. Of course, in order to attain this end, the subject should make a special effort to draw out the pure forms of conceptual beings and to allow them to obtain perfect independence and transcendence. Would this be successfully done if the original character of conceptual beings is retained?[1] As we have stated above, in order that culture may be essentially established as a realization or an expression of the subject, the selfhood and openness of the objects should be emphasized and the otherness and hiddenness be more suppressed. This is the precise function of contemplation. Its ultimate aim is, however, to conquer all otherness. And this will inevitably lead the contemplation itself and the subject as such to their own destruction. Therefore, to preserve an object, its otherness should be stressed. This can be done to begin with in the following manner. The subject tries to ascertain the otherness of an object by tracing the connection with natural life and existence back to its original source. In this case, the conceptual contents will regain their existence by becoming symbols of

---

1) Cf. *Philosophy of Religion*, § 16, 26.

the really existing others, nay rather by restoring their symbolizing power which they once had at the level of basic experience. Of course, this recovery is not a simple repetition. It is either an arrangement or development or expansion. The objective world of reality and its cognition are established in this procedure. This also happens in our daily life. But it is a function of learning or of academic study to accomplish it by some modification and to make possible its full achievement. The objective world of reality or simply the objective world which is dealt with by science is a product of an attempt to retain a relationship with natural life and existing reality by means of cognition. Accordingly " nature " as the object of science is a product of cultural activity, as Kant once observed. Although cultural activity has its root in natural life, it should be distinguished from it. But it is also true that some contents of objects do not denote any symbols of real others and, not belonging to the category of any real existence, still retain otherness in their own being. The objects of mathematical and logical thinking belong in this category.

Through cognition of the objective world of reality, the subject which still remains at the level of reflection re-enters the relationship with the reality of existence, from which it has once been estranged in the process of development. Now the fellowship with really existing being is the very ground or basis of our life, but how can reflection which has once abandoned this ground possibly restore it? This is possible because potentially reflection is contained in the basis of life. That is, reflection is not a sudden occurrence of something which is totally new. Reflection means that what has been potentially hidden in life freely exercises its proper function by coming to the surface and freeing itself from the control of others. As we have stated above, in some degree or other life involves culture in its reality and is furnished by a kind of experience. It is always accompanied by human awareness or cognition, no matter how inconspicuous they may be. This state of culture, however, is still wrapped up in the obscurity of natural life. When it is released, it steps onto the stage of reflection. Reflection as an act of freeing the subject should be related to the basis of life, from which it should be liberated. As this relationship with basic life is maintained, the subject can go back to that state. This act of tracing back is called " recollection " (or memory). And all our knowledge comes from this recollection. But it is not recollection as a kind of cognitive act which functions after actual cognition takes place. It is more basic. It is a necessary condition of cognition itself. So it should be called " transcendental recollection ", employing the Kantian terminology. Moreover, as a prerequisite to this recollection a connection of basic experience and reflection as well as an identity of the subject with both should be taken into consideration. Of course, this " transcendental identity " is disclosed and brought to consciousness only at the level of reflection or in the realization or expression of the subject. All attempts to seek for the identity of the subject or the selfhood directly, apart from the relationship or meaningful reference of the objective contents, will be proved vain.

Parallel to the cognition of the objective world, the subject also knows itself. As is stated above, objects are expressions of the subject and contain the factor of selfhood which is disclosed in them. The subject does not express itself except as object or in objects. This is the reason why the subject can know its own self. When the objects, that is, the expressions of the subject, become the symbols of the subject: that is, when the subject gets acquainted with its own self, and the hidden self or the center of the knowing act and the disclosed self or the known self are separated and opposed and, at the same time, maintain or realize their identity, the subject knows itself. From the standpoint of formal logic, one may say that this is quite impossible. But, since the objects which are separated from the subject at the level of reflection still maintain their significance as expressions of the self, this should be a quite natural conclusion. In this case, by the fact that the surface of objects is separated into the layers or fields of selfhood and otherness, expressions are developed into symbols and related to real existence (or the subject itself in this case) and thus they are transmuted into cognition. Those which in natural life symbolized real existence (or the others in this case) and formed the contents of the life of the real existence (or the subject) recover their meanings as contents of the life of real existing beings which symbolize real existence after isolating themselves in the form of objects. In this sense, we shall find again the act of transcendental recollection. But unlike the cognition of the objective world, the cognition of the self does not mean the restoration of any ideal being which has been a symbol of an other in basic experience. It rather takes an opposite direction and gains its seat as a symbol of the subject, and to that extent it means development rather than restoration. In relation to this we must give attention to the following two points: (1) This cognition takes place not only in the subject of natural life, but in the subject of every level of life; and (2) the cognition of the self as a liberation from natural life signifies a development. So that once it steps forward, it will proceed further in the isolation of objects of a higher grade through reflection at a higher level. There again we shall stand at a fork in the road. The right road will lead us to the higher level of the cognition of the self by means of this higher grade of reflection. Thus the beings belonging to the higher dimension, which were called by Plato "Ideas", become the subject-matter of self-cognition in the highest degree. Here the door will be open for viewing the whole structure of "philosophy" in its proper sense.[1]

More precisely, this is done in the following manner. As we have described it, the life which discloses itself at the level of reflection, still bearing the trait of activity, consists of two fields. From the fact that the objects which are others to the center of the subject nevertheless at the same time express the subject, it is required in the first place, that their identity involves two factors of selfhood and otherness, and

---

1) Cf. *Introduction to Philosophy of Religion,* esp. §§ 6, 16 seqq.

in the second place, that as the center of the subject becomes more active, the two fields which represent respectively selfhood and otherness will be separated and, at the same time, correlated. That is, the subject can act upon the objects only when it discloses itself in the form of objects. Of the two fields or two aspects the one represents that which acts upon or forms, and the other is that which is acted upon or formed. That is, the one is form; the other is matter. In reflection the subject, which constitutes the object of self-cognition, is also made of such factors. It goes without saying that in that case the aspect which stands on the side of otherness and matter represents real existence, and the aspect which stands on the side of selfhood and form represents its content. The real existence implies what is still hidden and the content refers to what has already been disclosed. Such factors are already furnished in the facts of daily life, but in science, especially in so-called human sciences, it will gain a more solid foundation and devolopment. Then how will this higher level of object that we have named higher degree of reflection become independent? It is achieved by separating the symbols which depend on selfhood and form from those which depend on otherness and matter, and stablizing them by establishing their independence (as is expected in reflection) and transcendence. These aspects, the pure forms which represent solely the factor of selfhood, will manifest the clearest appearance of life or its real being, which Plato called ὄντως ὄν or οὐσία. There the aspects which represent otherness will be left behind; so the irregularity and fluctuation on the phases of the objects will leave no trace and the obscurity of really existing beings will be dispersed, so that only the serene figure of being shining in its brightness will remain in the eyes of contemplation. This is the realm of philosophy. In the domain of cultural life, the deliverance from natural life will be achieved wholly by philosophy.

It is true that there is still a second possible way to achieve this aim. The intensification of the otherness of the object and the strengthening of its really existing character may also take place in these pure forms or pure objects. At least, it has happened several times in history, for instance in the metaphysics of idealism from Plato to Hegel.[1] In that tradition ideas are objects raised to a higher power and therefore, as such they refuse to be reduced to the really existing others of fundamental experience. So for them it is no longer possible to discern any meaning in them as symbols of real existence except as a higher self-cognition of the subject. Therefore, the thinkers who are unwilling to take the only right road to philosophy, and who are called dogmatists by Kant have no choice but to recline directly in the seat of reality. Thus the pure forms which have essentially no background nor depth, so that one can see to the bottom of them, are called reality. However different their inclinations and contents may be, these metaphysics all stand on a wrong foundation and over-step their competence.

### 3. Cultural Temporality

### (1)

In so far as the subject of pure contemplation ceaselessly expresses itself, conceals itself entirely in the object and does not disclose itself in any form of self-realization or activity, to that extent it is free from temporality. It is only in the cognition of the world of objective reality of existence which aims at the reestablishment of natural life and natural reality that the remanant of temporality can still be found. Thus an objective (or cosmic) time is established which is distinguished from historical time. As the subject will hide itself, it is not the time experienced by the subject, *i.e.* temporality as a character of the subject, but it is a temporality which comes into being only as an at-

1) Cf. *Philosophy of Religion*, esp. § 16, § 20.

tribute, form or law of the world of objects, *i.e.* of the objective world of reality. That is, it is not a time to be lived, but a time to be contemplated. This is the time or temporality by which we measure and talk about time and localize temporal events in our daily life. It is also the time of a chronometer or astronomy. In the respect that the subject stands in a close relationship with a part of the objective world of external reality and expresses itself in corporeality in its widest sense, it also exists or lives in this category of time. Unlike the case of cultural time or historical time in its strict and full sense, in objective time all the fluctuations and irregularities proper to the activity of the objects disappear and only their smooth surfaces remain. Objective time is often represented in the form of a straight line. It can be taken for a variation of cultural time or an extension of a segment of it just as a segment of a curve is taken for a straight line. But when the phase which represents otherness in historical or cultural life is attributed to its original source of really existing others, culture and history acquire the significance of constructing the objective world of reality as their substratum or basis and realizing or expressing themselves in it. So far historical time embraces objective time as its partical ingredient. But it will not effect an understanding of the structure of cultural, historical time as a whole. After much meandering, we are now obliged to step right into this matter.

## ( 2 )

As culture is built on the basis of natural life, cultural temporality is entirely influenced by natural temporality. Here, for a moment, we shall try to analyze its structure as we see it in its pure form undisturbed by the influence of natural time.

(a)  *The Present*

In cultural life the subject clings to its selfness (*shutaisei*: subjecticity) and retains its own self-assertion. Only others are estranged from natural reality and become objects. But the being of the objects is simply related to the subject and essentially they are found as potential self or self-expressions of the subject. So far the " future " (*shôrai*) and the " past " (*kako*) of basic natural time will disappear and only the " present " remains as the temporal characteristic of the subject. It may be safely said that the temporal feature of cultural life is exhausted in the present. The subject neither deplores the perished past nor bleats about the future which has not yet come; it simply enjoys the present in which it lives now at this moment. One can find its most typical example in aesthetic or theoretical contemplation, which endeavors to keep others in pure objectivity. From a temporal point of view, the pleasure of contemplating the beautiful or true image of a thing is that of enjoying the present.

Thus the " past " and the " future " in historical time are simply inner structures of the presentness of the subject which dominates and embraces all. Both of them obtain new meanings which are different from those in natural time.

### (b) *The Past*

It is the act of " recollection " (or memory) that renders new meaning and makes the " past " possible. The past as the content of recollection is a re-appearance of the being which was once reduced to nothingness. The word *kaisô* (recollection) is given not only to the act of re-appearance (*sai-gen*) but also to its content. In this case the being that is reestablished and exists in the present is merely an objective being. But one should pay special attention to the fact that there non-being is directed toward being and a being is awakened from nothingness; that is, the movement of being is entirely opposite that in natural time.

Several scientific explanations may be given to recollection as an empirical fact belonging or related to the world of objective reality. For example, it is caused by a certain influence or trance induced by some particular event. But even neglecting the fact that such an explanation presupposes the act of recollection, we must say that recollection is not a simple storing or retention of a changeless content, but refers to the recognition of its identity. But this requires again that the contents or objects of cognition belong to one single subject and that they are the expressions of the identical self. Recollection becomes possible when the subject advances to the level of the awareness of the self (*ego*) and lives in relation or opposition to its objects, *i.e.* when the subject advances to the stage of reflection and steps into the realm of freedom.

Of course, at the level of reflection or culture, its temporal aspect is exhausted in the present and all is reduced to being or entity. There is no nothingness in its strict sense. "Nothingness" (*mu*) and "non-being" (*hi-sonzai*) as the objective content of the present of the subject are themselves a kind of being or mode of being. Therefore, at the level of reflection which makes recollection possible, the latter comes into being as relationships or references of meaning between something in one mode of being and the same thing in another mode of being. But this is not enough to clarify the rôle of reflection which brings in the character of the past. It is only when a mode of being of nothingness at the level of reflection represents the nothingness in experience (of natural life, in this case) that recollection should be able to return to the original source and, consequently, be able to carry on transcendental recollection, as is mentioned above. But again as we have seen above, this is made possible by the fact that all the levels of life, and accordingly natural life, embrace the factor of reflection as a kind of experience. In other words, reflection does not mean a creation of being out of nothingness, but it means that something potential will become apparent. Of course, while we talk and think in this manner, we are obliged to stand at the level of reflection. And while distinguishing the factor of the life of experience, *i.e.* of real existence, from that of reflection, *i.e.* of ideal content, we establish a relationship of the two. So the former, *i.e.* the real existence, may also be introduced into the content of conceptual cognition. This is, however, the very difficulty one must face when he seeks for the source of experience. But it is a problem which one can no longer solve at the level of reflection. It is the very basic fact of life and there is no other way than to be in it and to live through it. A closer observation will show us that as we have seen in the cognition of the self, all the difficulties in identifying the hidden, really existing subject with the disclosed, ideal subject belong, after all, to the same category. They may all equally be reduced to what we call the transcendental identity of the subject. It is the identity of the subject of basic experience and that of reflection, in other words, the identity of the really existing subject and the subject which is expressed in reference to concepts in their objective phase. That is, it is the identity of cognizing subject (really existing subject) and the subject which is cognized (ideal, conceptual subject). Thus as this identity is primarily assumed as a prerequisite of reflection, it is not a matter of comprehension, but is a basic fact of life that should be experienced as we live through it.

Now recollection is re-appearance of the content which has once been reduced to nothingness. The real existence of its content has been buried in nothingness and there is no way of re-calling it. Its being re-appears as a concept. And of course, this is achieved by reflection. That is, recollection comes into being when conceptual being which is alienated and isolated from really existing being re-enters a special new being, while maintaining relationship and identity with the recollection. And it is by virtue of this recollection that the past in cultural time can be established.

The past thus established is comprised in the subject and its presence. It stands in a relationship with the subject and plays a special rôle as one of its moments or parts. That is, as a re-appearance or re-establishment of the being that has once been reduced to naught, the past supplies being to the subject at the level of reflection. The past maintains and supplies the being of objects to the subject and to that extent it represents material in which the subject is to be actualized. That is, the past represents the realm of otherness in cultural life as one of its temporal aspects. At the level of natural time the supplier of being was the future (*shôrai*). In cultural time it is the past that carries out the same office. As the otherness of objects is primarily originated in the otherness of really existing being, it is by means of the past that culture keeps its linkage with the world of real existence. Consequently, in a way we can say that here the direction of time is reversed. The past which meant perishing stands in the seat of the other and supplies being to the subject. It is an undeniable fact that here one finds a kind or a degree of liberation from the basic temporality of experience.

( c )  *The future*

In contrast to the past which represents the realm of otherness, the "future" (*shôrai*) represents that of selfness and form. The past is passive, whereas the future is active. The one is that which is acted upon; the other is that which acts. The subject receives its being from the past and tries to actualize itself or express itself by moulding what is given by means of the self which became manifest before it in the form of future. Here time flows from the past to the future via present.

Both the past and the future stand on the common ground of the present; indeed, they are rather entirely comprised in the unitary present or the identical self and come into being as the inner divisions or elements of the present. Both of them are different modes of being of the same present or the same self and are distinguished only by the difference of their modes of being. Thus a reciprocal relation of the two is established by means of the present. In the first place, the past as a supplier of being or a material to be formed which belongs to the realm of the otherness of objects, stipulates or conditions the act of the subject which achieves itself in it. And by doing so, it affects the future. It is because of the past that objects keep their relationship with the world of existence and the source of the past is existent others or the subject. Above all, the fellowship with existing others or objective nature which is retained and stabilized by cognition lies in the background of the past and helps particularly to strengthen its otherness. But after all this kind of nature also belongs to the objects. So it maintains cultural significance only as a potential self. And the past is also embraced in the present of the subject and governed by it. Therefore, in cultural or historical time the past which also comprises nature establishes itself only as a property of the self. History comes into being only when the subject which stands on the basis of its own past and makes use of it as given potentiality or material, realizes or expresses itself in or through it.

Although the same thing can be said of the past, the future also gains its meaning when it belongs to the subject. It corresponds to the realm of form and selfness in cultural life, and acts upon the past and moulds it by means of the present. The future is a world of freedom. It represents the factor of selfness in activity and stands particularly close to contemplation. The acting subject which seeks for the world of freedom foresees the coming reality in the future. This is a rôle of contemplation. Contemplation which is directed to the future as a moment of activity is ordinarily called " constructive thinking" (kôsô) or " imagination " (sôzô).

As recollection is to the past, so imagination is to the future. The past that stands on the side of otherness leads us to really existing being, especially to natural reality. Thus objective nature, that is, the objective world of reality which constitutes the subject-matter of natural science, strengthens the otherness of objects and builds up a solid background of the past. It should be said that recollection stands especially in a close relationship to natural science. On the contrary, the future and the corresponding imagination direct us to the way of philosophy. As we have already stated above, the objects of philosophy such as ideas and pure forms come into being when, in a process of the cognition of the self, the objective beings that represent selfness and form are liberated from those which represent otherness and materiality and are stabilized. When we rephrase it by the knowledge we have just had, we must say that imagination which is directed to the future is the very womb from which philosophy is born. In so far as it belongs to the future, object and imagination (which are produced from contemplation of the former) constitute only some part of the activity of the subject. When the aspects of materiality and otherness are abandoned and irregularity in the phase of objects become evened off and, by the development of the world of pure form, activity will surrender its place to contemplation, the future will be merged into the pure present and imagination, which has one of the factors of activity, will be developed into contemplation—intuition—of true being, that is, into the pure and calm form of being. From this it can be understood why, once it is related to activity, the " idea " which is the subject-matter of philosophy acquires an office of " ideal " and functions as a norm or value for the understanding of the reality of life. It is also easily envisaged that a road of development from natural science to philosophy is closed from the beginning. Natural science which aims at a return to natural life by emphasising otherness in the phase of objects takes a direction opposite to philosophy. Philosophy is an effort directed toward the future, whereas natural science is an effort toward the past.

The past and the future stand in a reciprocal relationship. Here we must pay special attention and emphasize the fact that the weight is more on the side of the future. In general this will be explained by the fact that the future which corresponds to the realm of selfness and form is much closer than the past to the essence of cultural life which intends liberation from natural life to the world of freedom. But if it is examined in detail, it is explained from the following concrete circumstance. The past which influences the future by means of the present in historical time comprises objective beings and is not pure other, but is simply that which corresponds to the moment of otherness in the field of the potential self and gives itself up to the disposal of the subject. Therefore from the beginning it has the character of the future and is colored and influenced by it. The past is always governed by the future. Of course, sheer fact or reality will reject any handling by the subject. But its content, that is, the being in its cultural sense, is conceptual being or being as meaning. Therefore, the past in history is not a simple established fact. It is a being which should be modified as the future changes. So far as the historical fact is called "historical", it is destined to sustain a flexibility which constantly modifies itself as the life of the subject changes. The recollection of the past incessantly gains new aspect and color as it develops, guided by the perspective of the future. In this manner, history is built in a reciprocal relation between the past and the future. And this relationship is achieved by means of the present under the predominance of the future. In history one always lives in a new future and, as a result, he lives also in a new past. There the past will cease to be something irretrievable, unchangeable and fatal.

( 3 )

So far, we have elucidated the characteristics of cultural time. There the subject and its " presence " dominates all. Both the past and the future, that is, the inner structures of the present, are comprised only of present, forming its parts or moments (elements). We have already seen that in natural time also the present embraces the past and the future in a certain sense. This comes inevitably from

40

the fact that time is originally considered as temporality, *i.e.* as a character of the subject. What is common to all the different degrees of temporality is that there the present occupies a predominant seat. But when we step out of this common ground, we shall find there several different ways to follow. In natural time the present, which borders on those which are others, always suffers from their pressure and intervention. That is, on the one hand, it is restricted by really existing others, and, on the other, it is obliged to perish into non-being. There the inner structure of the present denotes nothing other than its submission to this fatal necessity. In cultural life, however, these restrictions are removed and those who complained under the necessity and restriction of natural life will begin to enjoy freedom and liberation. Corresponding to this, the world of culture and objects becomes that of being only. There is no room for nothingness or non-being in its strict sense. The famous phrase of Parmenides, " What is thought is identical with what is," is a typical example which pointed out clearly and appropriately the nature of the cultural life. The past ceases to be a grave of being and is transformed into a source of being. Thus the current of time runs in reverse. It comes from the past, passes through the present and directs itself toward the future. Besides, as both the past and the future are nothing but special fields of the present, the flux of time remains in itself and neither comes from the outside nor disappears into the outside. When we follow this line of thought, there is no room for doubting that cultural or historical time is a certain form or degree of liberation or deliverance from temporality. But this is after all a liberation from " the past." And it can be achieved only when the past, giving up the absoluteness which it has once possessed in natural time, completely renews and remoulds itself and is modified by the subject, *i.e.* by the present and the future. So long as it stands under the influence of cultural or historical time, life bears a tinge of activity in its inner structure and is submitted to change and motion. Nevertheless life as a whole will know only living, not perishing. As far as life is furnished with the two aspects of form and selfness, on the one hand, and matter and otherness, on the other, and exists only as a fellowship of the two, the subject will enjoy the development of the changing future and rejoice in new expectation. It always stands on the basis of the enjoyment of the present, and a lovely melody of freedom and progress will add a dynamic color to it. Is there any happiness in this world which could be superior to this?

But after all, as cultural life stands on the basis of natural life and historical time is built on the foundation of natural time, they cannot get rid of the restrictions and influences of the basis upon which they are standing. The "present" which carries everything is perpetually submitted to incessant flow and change. The past which seems to emerge out of nothingness is held only by the present which incessantly sinks into nothingness. Life will not know perishing, only on condition that the present will last. Its constancy is nothing more than a rainbow which colors the spray of a waterfall. Apparently it may look peaceful and happy, but a closer examination of its content will show that the two factors of otherness and selfness, and accordingly the realms both of the past and the future, which are supplementing and supporting each other, at the same time, impede and reject each other, so that the aim of cultural being, *i.e.* self-realisation, always remains incomplete. Thus life always stays in want and never accomplishes itself. The ever-fresh and colorful relation between the past and the future will be simply an imaginary garment for concealing one's own self which is, after all, ever-perishing in self-destruction. Is not the philosophy of culture, *i.e.* humanism or secularism, nothing but the product of this self-deception?

# Chapter Three

# Objective Time

## (1)

Objective time is a simple variation of cultural time. It is a particular phase of temporality in the act of contemplation. But as in this stage the subject is hidden behind the object and remains only as an undisclosed center of activity, temporality has almost nothing to do with the subject. More precisely, as will be propounded in the following chapter, the most appropriate attitude for attaining this stage is to separate itself from temporality. But as we have already discussed, when contemplation takes the form of the cognition of the objective world of reality, in a certain degree it restores natural life. In more concrete terms, for the establishment of the cognition of really existing being, it is not enough to be satisfied with the observation of objective content and its relation. For example, as pure physics requires experiments, so one is obliged to meet and encounter real others and have a direct contact with nature. And where there remains any trait of the link with natural life, there remains also the character of temporality. Objective time comes into being in this manner. To the extent that a cognition of the objective world of real existence takes the form of contemplation, the subject retreats and its active nature disappears from the surface, so that its temporality may not belong to the nature of the subject, but simply to the nature of the world of objects. In order to understand the structure of this temporality, we should make clear the structure of the objective world of real existence and moreover, to achieve that end, we must know how this world has come into being.

As we have already discussed, the objective world of reality comes into being by relating objects with real others. That is to say, what has been enlarged through objects now obtains the center of its being and becomes their expression. Further in that case the new center comes up as a real other which stands in a real relationship with the subject. The object becomes an expression of a really existing other, which asserts or achieves itself in the former by disclosing its hidden center. In other words, the really existing other obtains its new seat as a subject in the face of the object. This is carried out by the cognitive act of the subject and so far it is based upon the act of the self-achievement of the subject and therefore it comes into being as a form of cultural life, but, on the other hand, as is stated above, it also means a return to the natural life. Thus when objects as self-expressions of the subject become the self-expressions of real others, the subject comes into a fellowship with real others at the level of culture. In the object the self-expression of the subject becomes one with that of real others and this means to render object a symbolic value and power. By " reality " (real existence) we mean a being which stands in a center and lives by it. That is, what really exists does not allow any other being to penetrate it, firmly defends itself against any invasion of others, nay even by invading others, it pushes itself to achieve its self-assertion. It the content of the life of the subject, which belongs to the self of the subject, does not indicate or represent any really other being, there is no way of communicating between the subject and others. Natural life is the most fundamental, direct, original and rudimentary form of such a fellowship with existing reality. In principle cultural life is characterized by the deliverance from this kind of primitive fellowship. But once this basic tendency is asserted to the end, all will fly away as if a meaningless dream or hallucination and the really existing subject will be dissolved into vanity. It is by virtue of the world of objective reality that this crisis is solved as it increases the phase of the otherness of the object. And this is achieved by some kind of return to the natural life. And as this return is made possible by means of cognition, we see thereby very clearly the important rôle that cognition plays at the level of cultural life. On the one hand, it carries the characteristic of contemplation and aims at the fulfilment of the essential tendency of cultural life, but, on the other hand, it saves the same life from its destruction by returning to the natural life and secures it a way of returning to its origin and prepares its sure foundation of reality. This is, however, carried out in our daily life. And as our cognitive act is elevated to a higher theoretical level, its original intention is accomplished.

From what has been said, it has become clear that the cognition of the objective world of reality bears an inevitably anthropomorphic character. Its direct object is ideal being which takes the form of object. And in principle it represents the subject itself. The subject knows others only through its own expressions. The existing others cannot penetrate us, ourselves, as such. Nevertheless, as that which belongs to us represents, at the same time, that which lies outside of us, our cognition is made possible. Unless a symbol of the other is formed in the subject through the unity of expressions of the subject and object, no cognition would be made possible. Here is the final ground of all the traditional theories which deny or doubt any validity to objective cognition. If we accept that the only way to reach the really existing being is to trace the relation of objective contents by reasoning and reflection, no matter how hard we try, we can never step out of the world of expressions, meanings and ideas and according to the terms of Leibnitz, we should end in being prisoners confined in a cell which is called a self, that " has no windows through which anything can come in and out," and thus we are inevitably inclined toward scepticism or conceptualism (idealism). Fortunately natural life furnishes to cognition the source of reality. We directly face or encounter really existing being and thus we get into an immediate fellowship with reality. Here the content of the life of the subject becomes a symbol of the other being and the self-expressions of the subject and others become identical. What renders such a basis of reality to cognition is this direct experience. The cognition of the objective world of reality is made possible by restoring such experiences and reestablishing the linkage with it.

So it is the basic fact of life which lies outside of our reasoning and doubt that the object which is an expression of the self is also a symbol of the other. But at the same time we cannot deny that the object which should be a symbol of the other clings to the realm of selfhood. The object in its proper phase as such has no connection with really existing others. Its essential tendency is rather to be freed from such connection. Of course, such a linkage is established and symbolism is formed by some fellowship with really existing being. Yet this new trait has not existed before at the level of cognition or reflection, but is attributed to it afterwards. Its proper nature as self-expression of the subject is not at all influenced by it. Consequently, in such a case, we can call it symbolism when that which keeps or preserves its own intrinsic character represents at the same time the other, or—when that which maintains its immanent character at the same time acquires its transcendence. Therefore, also in representations, those which express the others are formed only when those which express the subject are made their basis, materials or examples. As a result the others are represented in forms of person. Of course, in experience we hear the words of others directly. And we understand them simply by our own words or by the words of human being. So long as we actually live in this world, we must accept that personification is the inevitable fate of cognition and accordingly of all the phases of life which involve cognition as their factor. But by paying this price, we are allowed to go beyond the limit of the self and participate in the whole secret of being.

## ( 2 )

Here we shall not develop a detailed discussion on the basic forms of being, *i.e.* so-called categories of being in the objective world of reality. It is a very difficult task which lies beyond our competence. We shall limit the scope of our observation to the degree needed for the matter in question. Of the categories of the objective world of reality, the most important ones are substantiality and causality. Substantiality is, as is easily inferred from what we have mentioned above, nothing but selfhood (*shutaisei,* subjecticity or subjectness). Causality is formed when the relation between objects, *i.e.* the reference of meaning, is transferred into an actual relation of real existence. That is, when two objects or two groups of objects are related to each other, each respectively expressing meaning as real centers, causality comes into being. It symbolizes the relationship of the subject and the really other being. In this relationship the subject as center of life acts toward the outside but, at the same time, is acted upon from the outside. Activity and passivity are the double characteristics of the subject at the level of natural life. Corresponding to this, substances in the objective world of reality are both active and passive, reciprocally. Causality is formed as an interaction. We can say without exaggeration that the image of the objective world is patterned after the image of the human being.

But this is, of course, characteristic of the objective world of reality in so far as it exists as such. We have seen that the cognition of real existence becomes valid only by a certain degree of the restoration of the natural life. The natural life, however, rushes straight ahead toward others without looking about. It has a character quite contrary to contemplation which is the essence of cognition. Employing the terms of psychology, we can say that it works rather in a form of will or impulse than of intellect. Thus we are obliged to turn our eyes now to the dual structure of the knowledge of the objective world of reality. Seen from the original motive of contemplation as such, they should be overcome. The original objective of cognition will not be fulfiled until the rest of natural life becomes less and less or until the knowledge of the pure object is made possible. This is why in modern natural sciences it is necessary to alienate all personal images from sight and remove all factors implying selfhood. But this effort will bring fruit only to a certain extent. To take an example, even though we may be able to remove all the factors which denote the power or function of the subject, such conditions that imply outwardness, otherness or relationship may still remain, so far as the being outside of the self or the being which stands against it or their relationship still remains. This is the nature of space in its proper sense.

In order to understand "space", however, we must go back from objective space which constitutes the basic substructure of the objective world of reality to our basic experience, as in the case of time, and must examine the basic nature of space in natural life. As we have already seen, at the level of natural life the subject stands in a direct relation with really existing others. Here we can distinguish two aspects or factors: 1) the inner structure of the subject in a fellow-ship with others which is characterized by its temporality; 2) the phase of the subject so far as it directs itself toward others, *i.e.* its basic and proper phase as a being toward others. This is called spatiality. In short, the mode of the subject directed inwards is temporality and that directed outwards is spatiality. So spatiality which implies an inclination to face others or to exteriorize oneself is the most cardinal and basic outwardness or relativity.

Therefore, when natural life reestablishes its proper right to a certain degree, so that the objective world of reality may be rebuilt, space comes into being as its basic form. It is a natural consequence. The world of objects becomes real as it is linked with the subjective being which props them. The relationship of real existences must be spatial. All substances exist in space and the causality, *i. e.* their interaction, is carried out also in space. Thus spatiality comes to be the most basic stipulation of the objective world of reality. It is, however, true that spatiality can never claim priority to temporality, when it is traced back to the source of experience. Simply as a form of alienation or outwardization which is separated from the inner structure of the life of the subject, it cannot be otherwise than abstract and derivative in comparison to temporality. But as soon as an object is stabilized and actualized, as a real existence it begins to claim priority. In order to retain its selfhood to the end while the subject excludes any determination whatsoever which suggests its inner structure, it is simply obliged to follow such a way. That is to say, the spatiality of the objective world of reality comes from the character of its existing reality. It is understood as a spatial existence because it is represented to us in the form of a subject. By standing in relation between the subject and the really existing otherness, the object acquires subjective character as well as spatiality.

Thus, so long as the natural life dominates, there will be seen the rule of spatiality, too. It is true that, as conceptual being is formed, there comes into being a different kind of otherness, but it is also restricted by the yoke of spatiality. This is the reason why in order to express more concretely or allegorically the world of pure form or pure object or the world of eternity, one must represent it in some spatial images.[1] Even the very ideal world is described as a world " above ". Originally spatiality signifies really existing otherness in natural life which will be overcome by the formation of ideal being, but even in this new realm of self-accomplishment, as far as the self-

---

1) Although Plato distinguished εἶδος or ἰδέα from the "visible" (ὁρατόν) and called it the "intelligible" (νοητόν), originally it means "form" or "shape", *i.e.* it is something "visible" in higher degree. Even in the *"Republic"* (πολιτεία) where we find more strictly theoretical description, it exists in "a place or space which is intelligible" (ὁ νοητὸς τόπος) *(Rep.* 517 B). It is also accepted by many scholars that this view of Plato's left considerable influence on the thought of Plotinus and then on the chapter of *"Paradise"* in Dante's *Divine Comedy.* *(E. g.* Th. Whitaker. *The Neo-Platonists*, p. 199 ff.)

ness does not govern it, *i.e.* as far as it is laid under the influence of the otherness and the self is distinguished from the others, it is still related to the basic, original otherness. Therefore, it is quite natural that the objective world of reality which implies a return to the natural otherness is entirely subjected to the rule of spatiality. Here spatiality no longer serves as an allegorical expression, but manifests its power as an essential character of real existence itself. Thus it comes to constitute the most important factor of objective time, *i.e.* of the temporality of the objective world of reality.

## ( 3 )

Objective time comes up when the subject retreats from the stage of cultural time. As a consequence, there the irregularity and fluctuation on the surface of the object which are proper to activity will disappear and only such a time as plane, homogeneous, objective, cosmic form or order will be left. Of course, in the reality of life there is a strong tendency toward anthropomorphism and a subjective character is often attributed to an objective content, so that, corresponding to the form or degree of anthropomorphism, the structure of objective time also becomes rather complicated. For example, mutually interacting objective substances are represented as if each had its private temporality. Such a judgment to the effect that all things are perishable and subject to change is a product of anthropomorphism if we regard it as a judgment about the objective world of reality. The more the degree of cognition is developed, and the more anthropomorphism is suppressed and objectivity is confirmed, the firmer the stand of pure, homogeneous, and, so to speak, formal objective time which governs all things secures its solid foundation. Here both the past and the future disappear and only the homogeneous present presides. In such a present which has become homogeneous and equalized, otherness and relationship can be found only in terms of spatiality. If we still try to talk about time in this stage, it can be replaced by some spatial determinations such as length. There is no direction of time in the strict sense, *i.e.* no irreversibility of time. All changes and movements can be restored again. In fact, as is propounded by a certain scholar,[1] the fundamental rules of physics are quite unconcerned with the direction of time. It may be for specialists to decide whether it is right from the standpoint of natural science to reduce time entirely to a form of space and to establish a world of the fourth dimension. But there is no room for doubt that such a thought may be established as a result of the extreme objectivization of temporality.

But after all objective time is not the equivalent of space. It may not be represented without being spatialized or especially borrowing spatial images, but none the less it is still time. There the subject tends to hide itself in back, but never reduces itself to nothingness. So long as objective time is a variation of cultural time, the subject of cultural life and accordingly of natural life stands firmly behind it. Thanks to this fact, the all-inclusive homogeneous present which has no inner divisions moves or flows in a certain direction. Consequently the flow and transition of time becomes possible. But now that the inner structure of time in its strict sense, *i.e.* the rhythmic movement of the past and future, has already gone and is not retrievable, the flow and transition of time may be only a continuity of the present (now). One all-including present is divided into several small presents and thus there comes into being a time as an objective order of being which, although homogeneous, contains otherness in itself. So it should be said quite naturally that objective time is established only by the help of space which is the most fundamental order of the objective cosmic reality and is represented by spatial images. Thus as a continuity of points of time or nows (presents), it is represented as a line which is extended in a certain direction. The relation between the points of time is only external and spatial. It is only that the one is not the

---

1) Rf. Eddington, *The Nature of the Physical World*. P. 63 ff.

51

other or the one is contradictory to the other. As there is a certain direction, there is a distinction of the " before " and " after ". But even these are originally spatial determinations, as Aristotle long ago perceived.[1] It may be needless to say that " before " and " after " are quite different from past and future.

In objective time which is simply spatialized time, its inner structure is, just as in the case of space, sheer continuity or repetition of homogeneous identical content. The distinction between the one and the other is simply that they are others to each other and nothing more. If we go back further to the source of the question, we may be able to interpret it in the following manner: basic spatiality is the real otherness of existence in our basic experience. All otherness springs from this. As objects are isolated at the level of reflection, at the same time the objective, conceptual otherness comes into being. When the objective world is partly reestablished and, as it is isolated from the subject on this side, it is related to the real being, *i.e.* real others on the other side, the otherness comes up which is the objective space as the basic order of the objective world of reality. When all the characteristics which indicate reality are removed from objective space, the rest may be only otherness which is disclosed in the object or pure otherness which is formed in between the objective contents. This can also be applied to objective time. The otherness which governs it is simply the difference or otherness of the one and the other. That is, what distinguishes one " now " from another " now " is not their content. Therefore, from the outset it is denied that a now as an ultimate may have a special right to refuse the being of another now succeeding it. There is no limitation of any kind in such a continuity. That is, there can be neither beginning nor end. Indeed, unlike space, time is characterized by the fact that it takes a certain direction, so that endlessness is its most remarkable and essential character. This is the " endlessness " (*Endlosigkeit*) of time (*i.e.* of

---

1) *Physica*, 219a.

the objective time). In addition to this, the following point is also worth considering. On the side of the object where conceptual otherness governs, there is nothing except being. When one talks about nothingness (*mu*) in contrast to being (*yû*), the nothingness is but a kind of being, *i.e.* a different mode of being. If we apply this to time, there is only the present in objective time; nothingness in front of the present is merely another being, another present. That is, there is only a succession of presents, or nows. One cannot find there any real non-beingness, which can demand the cessation of this continuity. Where there is real otherness, the one annihilates the other or a being is reduced to naught. There nothingness (*mu*) *exists* in a strict sense. There the present can attain its end by becoming the past. Endlessness, therefore, should be said to be the most remarkable characteristic of objective time.

## (4)

It is undeniable that we can find here a certain degree of overcoming of temporality. Indeed, since ancient times the endlessness of objective time has been widely—and generally among common sense views—taken for the very eternity which implied the perfect overcoming of temporality. But this is an extremely erroneous interpretation. Objective time is not a time to be lived, but a time to be contemplated. Accordingly, it is true that at the level of objective time the subject retreats from the foreground of the stage, but it still continues to exist undisclosed behind the curtain. The subject of contemplation is also an acting subject. It even stands in the midst of the world of reality and acts in it, maintaining a connection with it. There the relationship between the subject and objective time comes into being. What does this endlessness of time or endless, infinite time mean, as we see it this way? It means the meaninglessness of activity. An infinite continuity of beings simply tells us the fact that being can never attain its fulfilment and perfection and that the self-realization of the subject can never be achieved. As it passes from one being to another, the subject always encounters the same being. And this being is always only the same potential being. Potentiality is nowhere actualized and will never be fulfilled. A linear being is after all a being without a center. As is already stated, the object has the subject at its center and it becomes meaningful when it realizes the responsibility of exteriorizing this center toward the surface. But here, on the contrary, we find simply a homogeneous continuity, an endless, linear duration of beings which have no center of the self to be actualized or expressed.

This will become much clearer once we trace it back to the original source of natural temporality. At the level of basic experience the present or the being is ever-perishing and evanescent. That which obtains its being will perish and that which comes into being will pass away. They are all unstable, fragmentary and privative. These are the basic characteristics of temporality. And when these characteristics come up to the phase of object, it is called endlessness. As each individual being is perishing, privative and unstable, it demands other beings and this claim will be made successively and knows no end. In other words, as at the stage of basic temporality being has an inseparable connection with nothingness, so at the level of objective time being will pass into another being which can be distinguished only by its being an " other ". In natural temporality being is encircled by non-being in its strict sense. Being is inseparably connected with nothingness, but nothingness stays outside of the being. As will be explained later, this is a characteristic of temporal, perishable present in contrast to the eternal present which involves in itself nothingness as a factor which has been overcome. This is the reason why the present and being are always replaced by the past and non-being. The connection of being and non-being that appears in the aspect of objects, is the endless continuity of beings. As has been stated several times, in cultural time or in objective time, all is included in the present. Time is the present and nothing else. Strictly speaking, there is neither non-being nor nothingness. They are rather different beings or another name for being. The non-being which lies outside of being and encircles it is nothing but another being which lies outside of the being and is connected with it superficially. The being and the present which essentially fall into non-being and past here become a being and a present which are essentially connected with another being or present. The corruptibility, inconstancy, unstableness, fragmentariness and incompleteness of being which are the basic characteristics of temporality are ultimately developed into an interminable continuity, called endlessness. In so far as a being neighboring upon a being replaces a being neighboring upon non-being, and as it means a shift from experience into concept, a certain degree of the overcoming of fundamental temporality is observed in this stage, but, on the other hand, so long as it perpetuates the defects of temporality, which have been several individual events, as endlessly continuous events, it is a sheer prolongation of the defects. Following the example of Hegel who called endlessness " bad infinity " we may be able to call this endless, limitless, objective time " bad eternity ", but seen from the fact that, although it looks like an overcoming of temporality, it is rather a prolongation of its defect, is not " false eternity " a more appropriate name for it?

Chapter Four

# Death

## ( 1 )

It is considered a noble prerogative of man to be able to think about death, especially to know its inevitability and to prepare for it. There are not many problems for those who reflect deeply about themselves which have as important an influence as the meaning of death. Moreover, it should not be confounded with such questions as in what manner death as an objective or natural phenomenon is related to life which is also an objective or natural phenomenon, or, more fundamentally speaking, how death as a natural phenomenon is accepted as an inevitable fact. Even if such inevitability could achieve a theoretical certainty, death as an unavoidable fact in this sense remains only an object of calm, theoretical observation which has principally no relationship whatsoever to the significance of the life which we are actually living. An objective study of the fact of death —especially the objective knowledge that all living beings (including ourselves) must die—may help us to apprehend the inevitability of death, so long as we are aware of the meaning of death even to a certain extent. Otherwise, it is even uncertain in what degree the phenomenon of death which is observed superficially is identical with the death which is our major concern. In certain cases, such kinds of observation or understanding will bring self-confidence or consolation from the simple and hasty deduction of exteriorizing the fact of death, and can even be an obstacle to achieving its more profound apprehension. The concept of death which was popular in Greek philosophy since Plato and had considerably influenced mediaeval and modern philosophical and religious thought—*i.e.* the notion of death defined as separation of mind (spirit) from body—should be counted as one of the remarkable examples of such an interpretation.

From this objective standpont, a Greek philosopher, Epicurus, tried to prove the foolishness of fearing death.[1] According to him, "death is after all a separation or dissipation of the atoms which constitute mind and body. So long as the unity of the two lasts, so that our existence continues, death is not present. But once death is present, we are no longer existing. For a living being, there is no death and the dead is naturally non-existent. To the extent that we have the power of perception, 'good' and 'bad' may have some meaning, but death is nothing but a total lack of perception..." Now, if we take the essence and significance of death as that which chiefly lies or is exhausted in something which is objectively examined and understood or in a phenomenon which belongs to the world of objective reality, it goes without saying that we do not meet our death in the same sense that we meet natural calamities. Nevertheless if we shun or fear it as bad luck in our life, even while thinking that we shall never meet it, it will be utter stupidity.—Such an interpretation of death, derives from a completely mistaken ground. It is not the encountering of an objective happening called death that we abhor or fear. We abhor and fear the fact that we ourselves should be reduced to non-being, or that we should not even come to encounter anything, not even death as an objective event.

It is true that death is not a matter of direct experience. So far as this point was made clear, what Epicurus said was right. Temporality is a structure of the direct experience in natural life. But that the present continually reduces itself into nothingness is not at all identical with death. In natural life, the subject which lives the present of each moment simply experiences its perishing, moment by moment.

---

1)   Rf. Diogenes Laertius, X, 124 seqq.—Titus Lucretius Carus, *De rerum natura,*
III, 830 seqq.

But death means a disappearance of the subject which has been and which will be identical all through the past and future, or a destruction of the present which comprehends the entirety of time. This can only be achieved at the level of cultural temporality. When the subject is raised to cultural life so that it gains the concepts of its own unity and totality, death is taken up as a problem. In natural life we find the present which represents each moment, but we shall find no present which covers all. Such an all-embracing present comes into being only as the subject expresses itself between or in connection with the objects.

## ( 2 )

But, as has been stated several times, nothingness (*mu*) in its strict sense does not exist in the cultural consciousness. Therefore, so far as we are standing on the basis of cultural philosophy, we are totally engaged in the all-embracing present and are negligent in tracing back the basic origin of life itself, so that death as well as nothingness can never come into being in its exact sense. Spinoza declared from the depth of this thoroughgoing cultural awareness, " Free men (the wise and experienced) scarcely think of death. Their wisdom is not a meditation of death, but of life."[1] Modern ethnology has disclosed the interesting fact that there is very little notion of death among uncivilized primitive people. " For them it is a self-evident fact that a living being continues to live endlessly. It is rather difficult for them to understand that life must end with death. Among them it is often observed that not only people who are well-off, but the entire race or tribe as well are thought to be transferred into paradise as they continue to live. For them death is rather an unnatural thing that requires special explanation. Even after they are convinced of the inevitability of death, they do not think of death as the termination of life, but

---

1) *Ethica*, IV, 67.

simply as a continuity of life in a different form. For them death is only a special mode of living. Also they interpret their mode of living in such a way that the distinction between life and death is largely wiped away. That is, the dead continues to live in his entirety (not in part such as a soul or a spirit, and even when they used this word, its meaning was different from the same word employed by later thinkers), in the same body and form that he used to inhabit or that he had at the moment of his death. In some cases it is simply believed that the dead may become lighter and thinner like a shadow or smoke, as some people today still believe in the existence of ghosts..."[1]

This may be easily interpreted as the most faithful reflection of basic experience which is found in the simple and naive thoughts of the races which are called natural or primitive men. Of course, we cannot deny that the daily awareness of those races is very deeply colored by the so-called natural and basic experience, their cultural awareness is not strongly expressed, and as a result the content of their culture still remains in a primitive stage of low grade. But nevertheless they have a certain culture of their own. Their reflection on the basic experience is an achievement of cultural men and therefore whether their reflections and interpretations (*i.e.* the expressions of their reflections) are appropriate or not should not be decided simply from the fact that their average daily awareness has some trait of comparatively primitive basic experience. In short, their idea of death comes rather from their cultural awareness and no matter how primitive or immature it may be, it proves that they are standing at the level of culture. As far as they think only of life and do not think of death, they stand on the same footing as that of a modern great thinker, Spinoza. The only difference will be that, while the latter has driven

---

1) Cf. Ankermann. *Die Religion der Natur-völker* (Bertholet-Lehmann, *Lehrbuch der Religionsgeschichte*. Bd. I.) —Preuss, *Tod und Unsterblichkeit im Glauben der Naturvölker* (1930), Walter Otto, *Die Manen* (1923). The last chapter of this book has the merit of revising the interpretation of Rohde on the notion of the dead among the pre-historic Greeks. Also see Lévy-Bruhl, *Les fonctions mentals dans les sociétés inférieurs*. p. 416 (Engl. tr. p. 353).

home the theory of culture more philosophically through deep self-reflection, they live it just simply and innocently. As cultural life looks at only being and not nothingness, and as from the standpoint of temporality the present swallows up both the past and the future, so there exists simply life, not death. Therefore, even if they begin to understand the presence and meaning of death to a certain extent, they simply take death for a kind of life. Recent study[1] has made it clear that the philosophy of regarding death as a separation of mind and body, as Rohde thought under animistic influence,[2] is not a common aspect relating primitive folks and Plato. Omitting reference to the great difference between primitive folk-thought and Plato (especially the incomparable depth of the self-reflection of the latter), we notice a considerable distance between the two in the simple understanding of the essence of death. Yet we must nevertheless say that both are completely identical in so far as they regard death as a mode of life. And this corresponding point is nothing but the inevitable manifestation of cultural philosophy itself. The men of culture, who are themselves entirely given to the present and are not aware of the fact that their foothold is all the time trembling and disappearing into non-being, ignore or dislike to face the reality of death and indulge in intellectual or sentimental contentment of illusion which regards death as a kind of life. The fact that, through all ages, races, social classes and cultural types, this thought has prevailed within the entire human world—*e.g.* in the view of immortality or transmigration of soul, or in ideas of reward and punishment, or as a factor of deliverance and salvation, or in a simple and naive belief or in a complicated profound theory of speculation—will tell us how deeply it is rooted in the hear of human nature. Unfortunately it is an erroneous thought which considers man as an existence with brain but with no body to sustain or intestines to nourish him. In a sense it is even self-deception.

1) Rf. W. Otto, *Die Manen.*
2) Erwin Rohde, *Psyche.*

## ( 3 )

In brief, it is indeed at the level of culture that we shall have a real concern and apprehension, even the very concept of death, but we shall never grasp its true picture so long as we remain in this stage. Strictly speaking, in the field of culture we shall find only life, not death. Thus we are obliged to turn our eyes further to the deep origin of the matter and to go back to the natural life, that is, to the basic experience of temporality. Death is not a matter of our immediate experience, but nevertheless only by turning our reflection to the direct experience of temporality, shall we find and understand it as a matter of particular importance with a special meaning of its own.

When we seek after the extremity of natural temporality or the irreversibility of time, there we shall find " death ". Death means the corruption or annihilation not only of each present but of the whole present (or presence) , *i.e.* of life. For the subject which exists as an orderly whole, death means an extinction of a link with all existing others and therefore a complete negation of the future in its basic sense. Death is a subject which has lost its object or a life without future. We have already seen that in original temporality the present loses its being in the past, but it is supplied immediately from the future. It is because of the future and the connection with others that, despite the fact that the present passes incessantly into non-being, it always regains itself in new being. The present which has no route for supplying its being, which has fallen into an absolute solitude or the life which only passes away and has no hope of welcoming what is about to come, has no other choice than to die. Death signifies an entire, thoroughgoing destruction of the subject.

As is stated above, we cannot directly experience death of such a nature. It is apprehended as an essential nature of the existence of the subject who tries to understand himself in his entirety. Since in so far as we are living we do not meet death, it is always found as a possibility. Moreover, its essential character lies in the fact that it is not a possibility which, as a factor of the self-achievement of the subject, depends on his free will, but a possibility which has originated in the relationship with existing others. We have seen that temporality is an inevitable and fatal phenomenon which, whether one likes it or not, governs the existence of the subject. In death which is an extreme manifestation of temporality, this inevitable and fatal character also takes an extreme form. It eats into the deepest hidden core of the subject and entirely destroys its existence and its selfhood. But since it is given as a possibility or tendency which forms the essential nature of the subject, it is a matter that we must accept as a destiny we must some time face. And also because of that, there is room for taking an attitude which considers it a matter that can be avoided either theoretically or practically, or by interpretation or action. On the one hand, death is an extreme deepening of temporality and is closely related to our basic experience; but, on the other hand, it can be found only at the level of cultural life. This is why the reality of death which is furnished with necessity and possibility at the same time is so difficult and complicated to apprehend. But once we attain the reality of death by tracing it back to the basis of experience, we shall understand it simply and easily as a very meaningful and essential factor of human nature. Human existence is an existence toward death. It is the duty of death to awaken the sweet dream of a man of humanism who enjoys his life and present (presence) and to let him know his true being and reality. To a man who is transported by the nectar of humanity, nothingness means only another kind of being. It is the word of admonition, "Don't forget death!", which teaches him that being cannot overcome non-being, that at non-being being will reach the limit which cannot be surpassed, and to make him aware of the solemn reality of life. The wise in Spinoza thinks only of his life, but the truly wise will surely think of his death as well as his life.

As we have seen, the meaning of death is disclosed when the cultural subject realizes the subject of natural life to be its basic foundation. We have often made it clear that, in regard to the cognitions of the objectively real world and the subjective self, or concerning cultural temporality, there should be a transcendental identity of the subjects of reflection and experience as their necessary condition. But it will become clear that the same identity also forms a *sine qua non* for the understanding of the concept of death. Indeed, it is even necessary for us to accept the transcendental identity of the subject in its most basic and original form. Of course, in other cases too it is observed that natural life and its self-assertion form a basis or foundation of all kinds and aspects of human life, but they will never approach so closely and strongly to the heart of our life as in the notion of death.

Death is an effectuation of temporality. Therefore, temporality can be overcome only by conquering death and, contrariwise, the conquering of death is accomplished only by that of temporality. From this we can draw the following conclusions: 1) We think very often that temporality and the annoyance of this world derived from it might be solved by death itself. It should be said quite naturally that this kind of thought or feeling has a strong influence among the average population, if we think how deeply we are also affected by the thought of considering death as a kind of life. But it has already been made clear from the preceding passages that it is a complete illusion. Of course, we must say that such a thought has some ground of its own. Death as a separation from others surely means for the subject to pass away from this world. In a certain sense, death surely is a deliverance of the soul from temporality and all the sufferings of this world. Unfortunately this deliverance signifies at the same time the destruction of the subject himself who should have been delivered from death. If all the sufferings of this world derive from the oppression and denial of the self-assertion of the subject, death may be said to be an aggravation of the suffering in this world. Viewed in this light, we should take the sufferings of this world rather for the omens or harbingers of death.

2) We know that eternity which is the overcoming of temporality should be, at the same time, the overcoming of death, and the overcoming of death can only be achieved in eternity. From this, it is also clear that the notion of immortality as a simple continuity of life is not satisfactory for an answer to the need for conquering death. The orientation for attaining a true understanding of eternity is already suggested here. If death means the losing of the future of the subject, eternity is the present which has no past, but only the future. In connection with this, whereas death is a complete separation from others, eternity must be a perfect fellowship of life with others. Solitude means death, but eternity comes into being only as love.

# Chapter Five

# Immortality and Endlessness

## ( 1 )

As we have often stated, in each field of temporality we already find some kind of solution for overcoming it. Natural temporality, which is the root and source of all the temporalities, transforms itself into cultural temporality, but this transformation implies some modification. The temporality of cultural life is characterized by its ever-presentness. To the extent that culture dominates, there are only beings and the present. The past which has been a grave of beings in the basic experience here becomes the very womb of being. So far as one lives in the domain of this temporality, no one knows perishing. The subject who enjoys the present and anticipates the future lives in the actualization of its being.

But when we seek for its foundation, we shall find that this lovely world of activity, enjoyment and hope is simply a castle built upon sand. The present which is supposed to carry and support beings as a whole incessantly passes away into destruction. Also it is a being which depends upon the future, *i.e.* upon others. The perfect effectuation of this character of temporality is death itself. The most tragic phase of humanity lies in this fatal fact of death, *i.e.* in its possibility which is furnished with necessity or by force. Thus the overcoming of temporality should be the overcoming of death. Eternity should be found in the form of immortality.

Since Plato immortality (*Unsterblichkeit*) has been known as the deathlessness or imperishableness of the " soul ". But in spite of the glorious and old tradition of the concept, its connotation is extremely ambiguous and lacks academic exactitude in usage. The conceptions of both " soul " and " immortality " are found even among primitive races, and even after they became objects of academic study or theoretical observation, they have been made quite complicated and obscure, by virtue not only of differences in philosophical points of view, but also of the influence of popular interpretations. But at the same time this obscurity comes particularly from the lack of basic methodologicial reflection on the study of temporality or from the superficial apprehension of the subject-matter. Many great philosophers have dealt with these themes for a long time. But no theories so lack persuasive power as does the concept of the immortality of the soul. For example, let us review some of the theories which are historically important. In opening Plato's book of the *Phaedo,* although it is written for the sake of proving the immortality of the soul, the substantiation of the theory, as Plato himself confessed, is theoretically very weak and to our surprise its main significance and value lie rather in several doctrines which are used primarily as materials for the argument, especially the doctrine of ideas. In spite of its celebrity and its ostensible use of the plot and characters of Plato, the book by Mendelssohn which has the same title, was only an imitative adaptation applied to thought current in the age of enlightenment. Its significance was not philosophical but literary. Kant, whom Mendelssohn called " a destroyer of everything " and who actually destroyed the current belief in the immortality of the soul represented by Mendelssohn, proposed in its place a new demonstration of the immortality of the soul on the basis of " a postulate of the practical reason." Despite the fact that a strong belief and cosmic theory are latent in its background, Kant's demonstration itself is very loose. It is surprising to see the same author who wrote the " Critique of the Pure Reason," where he attempted the destruction of all the metaphysical notions of the " soul " (*Seele*) and strongly propagated the super-temporal character of true reality, propounding a solution of

66

the problem of the endless or temporal continuity of the soul by means of the "postulate". According to his explanation, although its ground is guided by practical laws, the proposition itself should nevertheless be theoretical.

To the extent that one cannot treat death as a matter of objective cognition, immorality should be expounded from the standpoint of the understanding of the self and can come into being only as faith. It is basically wrong to treat it as if it could be theoretically founded. In this study we must trace this understanding and belief in ourselves back into their sources in life, if possible, and by disclosing its reality, we must attain a correct understanding of them. Of course, we shall also be critical. But it should be critique as understanding. That is, it should arise from the problem itself, or, in this case, from the very nature of immortality and its original intention or meaning.

( 2 )

In most cases, "spirit", "soul" and words of a similar connotation have been used with reference to death.[1] As we have seen, among primitive people there is the faith that it is the whole and not simply a part of a man that survives after death. It may be either the corpse itself or the man himself who is in some sense identical with the corpse, although the "soul" remains a separate being along side the corpse.[2] Even as it has been separated from the corpse—as is obviously the case in cremation—, the spirit or soul is always con-

---

1) See p. 60 note 1. Also see Er. Rohde, *Psyche*. J. Burnet, *The Socratic Doctrine of the Soul* (Essays and addresses, p. 126 ff.)

2) It is a general tendency found in the thought of primitive races to regard those who are related as identical. Thanks to the study of Lévy-Bruhl this point was made clear. But the fact that he called it *mentalité prélogique"* shows that, rather contrary to his own assertion, he is bound to be in the European tradition of thinking. The simple fact that a way of thinking is extremely different from, or in some cases contrary to that of contemporary cultural people does not necessarily mean that it is *"prélogique"*. If it is allowed to exaggerate a little, it is similar to the case of Hegelians who may call the logic of Aristotle or Kant a *"mentalité prélogique."*

sidered as the entire man. Take for example the case of the ancient Greeks who had fortuitously a promising future in developing an almost unique form of thought. What is called *psyche* (ψυχή) in the Homeric poetry is such a kind of spirit or soul. It is the dead man himself and not simply a part of him which was separated from or came out of his former being, but a vital power which administers the life of living man is distinguished from it. Homer called it *thymos* ( θυμός ) which is related to or identified with his blood or breath. It perishes and will be gone somewhere at the moment of death and have no relationship with the man and his soul. Primitive thinking has a characteristic of not relating the soul with the life before death. In such a stage it is more likely that the actually living subject may engage in deep self-reflection about his own death or his destiny after death. There death is treated as an objective event. And as this objective event happens also to himself, his existence after death will become a concern of the living. Achilles exclaimed that he would rather be a poor tenant farmer who cultivates the land of the poor than be the king of Hades.[1] Such turning of their thoughts, even negatively, to their existence after death might have been a common thing. But it would not be one's own destiny that is taken up in such observations of existence after death. They are made rather only in relation to other people, or in respect of the good or bad influences which would affect the survivors. For the living it is more important to think of the attitude he should take in the face of the dead, that is, toward the soul of others, than to think about one's own destiny after death. It was perhaps in the Ionic philosophy that the soul was thus related to the life of the living and acquired significance as a power or principle of life. Obviously it was taken from Homer's θυμός and was renamed ψυχή from a scientific point of view. But it is very significant in the history of thought that a name which had been used to identify a being after death was applied to that which

---

1) *Od.* XI, 489.

administered living beings. It was a further advance that, in Socrates, life which is administered by the soul became an object of wisdom, truth and morals. That is, the soul became the subject of cultural life. But he who believed it his calling to develop cultural awareness in people neither talked nor gave much concern to destiny after death. That should be the natural consequence of the essence of cultural temporality. As is well known, it was Plato who took the last step forward which was necessary to attain this stage. It was the influence of Orphism that enabled him to reach that point. In this religious group the main subject of concern was the destiny of human life after death. The way to reach that stage had not been very easy and the subject-matter had not been very simple. The most conspicuous factor in its argument is its claim to the identity of the subject of life before and after death. This identical subject embodies the very notion of " soul " (ψυχή) which was adopted by the animistic theory prevailing for some time among scholars, especially in the philosophy of Rohde, and was considered a concept commonly found among primitive races. In this case the soul of the living is simply a prolongation backward of the soul of the dead. Above all, Orphism interprets the soul as a divine being which once lived in a higher world, descended temporarily into a human body where it sought its dwelling-place. Their main concern was, therefore, not the fate of the human subject living in the present, but that of a foreign parasite which reaches or returns to its native place only when death arrives. Or, in some cases, it was the fate of the soul which was regarded as a kind of mythical being that had nothing to do with the actual life. It has some important meaning that although Plato was greatly influenced by the thought of the day, he still kept standing in the tradition of philosophy and concentrated on the problem of the soul of the subject who actually lives or exists, especially of the subject of cultural life. Because of his effort, the existing and living human subject became a real subject concerned about the immortality of soul as his own fatal fact. Immortality has been a subject of philosophy ever since. The Orphic influence, however, together with Plato's idealism which gave more importance to cultural life, contributed to an extreme alienation of the soul and the body. As a result, death and the life after death became not the subject of man as a whole, but of the soul as forming merely a part of man. In general, since the time of primitive people, the objectivism which tends to regard death as an event of the objective world, interprets it as a separation of mind and body and, by doing so, encourages the tendency of dealing with only a part of the soul. After Plato there appeared a considerable number of theories on the soul in the course of history, but most of the important expositions of the meaning of the soul had been given in the studies of Plato and his predecessors. In general (and especially in academic study), the word "soul" was used synonymously with "mind" or "spirit". That is, on the one hand, it meant the dead, but, on the other hand, it was a power which administers life or the subject of life. And thus when one sees it in relation to life, one must say that it constitutes the most essential part of man, although essentially it does not at all mean a "man in his entirety". Such characteristics of a word, which has already been rather ambiguous in its connotations, makes us more sceptical about its validity as an academic term. The theme of our discussion is how a human subject can overcome temporality and death and how he can have an experience of eternity. So-called immortality of the soul is worth considering only when it is related with these problems or included in them. Under such circumstances, although we must pay our respects to this old and venerable tradition, we are obliged to keep this conception or terminology outside our philosophical or theoretical discussions.

As is already stated, when primitive people showed their concern about death, they meant thereby a special mode of being or life. Of course, the notion of immortality can already be found there in embryo, but it is not developed. In some cases the soul which continues to exist after death may gradually disappear when, for example, a mass for the dead which was observed by the living ceases. The notion of immortality gains its significance only when temporality which is the source of death is overcome basically in some way or other. It can be observed even in objective temporality. It is a variation of cultural temporality. But although through activity which is intrinsic to cultural life selfhood is disclosed in a particular form or field in the aspect of objects, here the separation from the subject is undertaken in principle, regardless of its possibility. As a consequence, time is extended in infinitude, and "endlessness" constitutes the character of temporality. The immortality which signifies eternity should, in the first place, take this form. Indeed, this is the very idea of immortality which has actually been adopted in the main current of thought by many philosophers from Plato to Kant.

( 3 )

Already in the time of Democritus and Plato the question of the beginning and end of time had been raised. The question is inferred in the writings of Aristotle.[1] In most of the cases we see it in their philosophy the question generally arises in the framework of cosmology or natural philosophy with regard to the world and its contents. Consequently it was quite natural that Augustine, Thomas Aquinas and other Mediaeval European thinkers held the same view, understanding from their religious standpoint that the being of the whole world is limited at both ends of time, at creation and at the end of the world. Kant also dealt indirectly with this problem in his first antinomy. This is again related to the cosmological theme of the beginning and end of the world. It is true that the conception of an empty time (*die leere Zeit*) is simply a product of

---

1) *Physica*, 251 b.

logical abstraction, and essentially time exists in actuality only as an intrinsic structure, order or a form of some existing being or content. Therefore, it is not without foundations that such traditional views were found in the course of history. But we must not forget to see the true and essential aspect of time by tracing it back to the source of our experience. By doing so, we shall not be bothered by any false conceptions of theories or doctrines which have almost nothing to do with the nature of time as such. Many people simply discuss the beginning and end of time, assuming objective time as something self-evident which does not need to be examined. This is a wrong approach to the question. That is to say, we must first of all understand time as a mode of life or temporality, by relating it to the subject and its original mode of life. And after analysing the fundamental reality of time and temporality, we must try to discover its various strata or grades. As mentioned above, Augustine and Bergson are the two great pioneers who led us in this right direction. But it is our own task to discover the way to follow.

Our own answer, however, has already been given in the preceding chapter where we discussed objective time. We consider endlessness to be the temporal character of the objective world of reality. This does not mean, however, that time takes on an absolute character when it is extended limitlessly, as Kant feared. Life may proceed into a new or higher stage, or more precisely speaking, eternity may appear in the midst of life. Temporality as well as the endlessness of time, however, will be thereby restricted and resolved (overcome). But in so far as cultural human life which is built on natural life continues to exercise its power, the endlessness of time may also remain valid.

We have already emphasized that endlessness does not mean any overcoming of temporality and that it is rather an extension of perishableness or fragmentariness which forms the essential character of fundamental (original) temporality. To the extent that the concept of immortality is built upon this endlessness which we have called " bad or false eternity ", it is easily observed that this concept will lose its basis and inevitably fall down. Therefore, the immortality which means endlessness is no solution of temporality and no overcoming of death. It is merely an illusory conception that is apt to be held by a cultural subject which has forgotten its origin and basis. Unless the original fundamental temporality is resolved, death cannot be overcome, either. Then where does this illusion come from? It comes from a false understanding of death. It comes from ignorance of the fact that death is a thoroughgoing effectuation of temporality which means extermination or falling into nothingness. In other words, death is interpreted objectively as an event in the objective world of reality. If one assumed that time is the equivalent of objective temporality, he would see only a continuity of beings or nows, as we have stated above. Death would simply mean a transition from one being to another. Regardless of the detail of the content, in substance death would be simply a modification of being. Consequently the subject which may meet death would simply fear death itself, not the annihilation of his being. If death ought to be feared, the fear should arise from some other cause or reason. Therefore, for those who seek or believe in eternity and immortality, the most pressing need would be that such cause or reason for the annihilation of being would not exist, or, more positively stated, some cause or reason which makes life continue endlessly should be found.

( 4 )

This will give us new guidance for understanding the significance of arguments about the so-called immortality of the soul which have been developed in the course of the long history since Plato. From a purely theoretical point of view, one can say that these demonstrations stand on extremely weak grounds or inferences. But the thoughts or beliefs that lie behind them and support them and that give them life have sprung from the basic source of life. They have their own particular *raisons d'être*. Let us take up two of the most typical and influential examples and give them the names of "ontological" and "teleological" demonstrations. The ontological demonstration starts from the real being or essential nature of the soul or, more correctly speaking, of the subject himself and in principle it gives no consideration to his fellowship with others. On the other hand, the object of the teleological demonstration is a subject which exists and lives in this world, that is, which stands in relation to others.

From Plato and Plotinus in the classical period, Thomas Aquinas in the middle ages, up to the modern theories of Leibnitz and Mendelssohn,[1] the most dominant thought on the ontological demonstration has been based on the simplicity of the subject. Unlike the material body which exists spatially and therefore is complex and consists of beings meeting at their outer surfaces, the soul is simple and gives unity to the complexity of objects. Therefore, it is never dissolved into constituent elements and thus never perishes. This is the main reasoning in their arguments. When we ignore the theoretical value of the parts and of the whole and trace back to the origin of these thoughts, we shall find that they derive from the notion of the simplicity, or the selfhood of the subject. The selfhood of the subject which confers meanings and contexts to all objective beings is itself simple, but, on the contrary, the objects stand on the side of others and involve in themselves otherness, that is, differences and plurality. So they are complex and plural. For instance, once the subject is alienated in its pure selfhood from a real other, suspending the context of objects, and providing a new content and a new context from which objectivity and real otherness in general derive, there would be nothing but selfhood, its being, and the present

---

1) Plato, *Paidon*. 78.—Plotin, *Enneades*. IV, 7. Thomas Aquinas, *Contra Gen-*. *tiles*. II, 55. Leibnitz, *Monadologic*. Mendelssohn, *Phädon*. Zweites Gespräch. (Gesamte Schriften, Jubiläumsausg. III, S. 78 ff.)

as its temporal character. As we have often observed, this is the objective of cultural temporality. But we have also stressed in several passages that the selfhood which is alienated from otherness occupies no place in the life of human existence. Cultural life is an achievement of the self in others, that is, in objects and their relationships and, at the same time, it stands on the basis of natural life. But the subject of natural life or the subject in its most fundamental sense which bears all aspects of life is found only in relationship and fellowship with real others. If the subject were able to assert itself and its being to the end, or if it were found in its pure and simple selfhood, it would never perish, so that the aim of the ontological proof might be realized. But it would be entirely a matter of imagination and phantasy. Natural life which is the source and basis of all the aspects of life is essentially characterized by its temporal corruptibility. The intrinsic objective of cultural life is to overcome this temporal corruptibility and there one might find some development in this direction, but it is essentially impossible to achieve this aim. It comes from the fact that the subject can never exist in its pure simplicity. It is thanks to the fellowship with others that the assertiveness of the subject can be actualized.

( 5 )

Unlike the proof from ontology, the teleological proof seeks for its ground in the relationship of the subject with others. Thereby the subject in question is also the cultural subject. In the case of the ontological proof, this subject is treated as a simple and pure power which governs all in its pure selfhood and even when others are taken into consideration, they are regarded as pure and accomplished expressions of the subject. That is, otherness is treated as almost equal to nothing over against selfhood. In the instance of the teleological demonstration, however, others are seriously taken into account. First of all, others are objects, and they are further the objective world of reality where objects are reduced to real others. In short, here the subject is treated as a being-in-the-world (*In-der-Welt-sein*). The subject which is envisaged from such a point of view is a dynamic center or origin of an act of realizing itself in others. As is stated above, activity is its basic character. It is not without reason that in modern philosophy which has been characterized by grasping cultural life in this aspect, this kind of reasoning and the conviction which works as a dynamic factor for it have made remarkable progress. The obvious expressions of these thoughts or demonstrations can be found in the philosophy of the epoch of enlightenment such as of Kant, Lessing, Lotze and others, but as a mood or sentiment, or as longing or belief, such a thought played a dynamic rôle in motivating modern philosophy since the Renaissance.[1] From the most popular pan-humanistic desire of establishing an incorruptible name to be delivered to later generations, all the way to the deepest philosophies of Kantian "Reason" (*Vernunft*), Fichtean "Ego" (*Das Ich*), Hegelian "Mind" (*Geist*), wherever the value, superiority and dignity of the cultural subject are felt, understood or believed, one can find some signs of teleological reasoning even if only in embryonic form.

It would be interesting to compare those different types of philosophy from an historical point of view, but it would be far from our original assignment. What we are intending here is to explore the basic thoughts which lie behind them, leading them to the concep-

---

1) Mendelssohn, *Phädon*. Drittes Gespräch. Kant, *Kritik der praktischen Vernunft*. Ak-ausg. S. 122 ff. Lessing *Erziehung des Menschengeschlechts*. Lotze, *Mikrokosmos*. 3Bd. III. S. 74 ff. It is interesting to point out the similarity and differences among these thinkers. Let us take the last two for example. They both maintained that the life after death has a connection with the present life and both the dead and alive live a common life. They laid the foundation of their thoughts upon the postulate that the subject itself should experience an accomplishment of its aim; but Lessing tried to reestablish the notion of transmigration of the soul, whereas Lotze is satisfied with the connection between this world and the other world. It is also interesting to note that, in a certain sense, both of them reverted to the thought of primitive people.

tions of immortality and endless being and to apprehend and examine them critically from the fundamental nature of life. Teleological proof starts from the self-realization and activity which are the fundamental characters of the cultural subject, and deduces the endlessness of life as a necessary condition for its accomplishment, that is, for the realization of the final purpose of the subject. This accomplishment is represented either as " perfection " (*Vollkommenheit*) or the highest good (*Das höchste Gut*) or as happiness. Of course, there are some differences among them. For example, there is not a little distance between the Kantian conception of the highest good which is based upon the notion of unconditional ethical value and the ideas of happiness and perfection which prevailed among the thinkers of the period of enlightenment which was approximately the epoch of Kant, but in principle they all held the same view. Here the kind of activity does not come into our consideration. Even contemplation is taken into account in respect of its active aspect. Moral duty (*Sollen*) is also regarded as an activity of the self-assertion of the subject and as an act of will which constitutes the actual nature of the subject. In this respect one finds some interesting themes in the philosophy of Kant. " The highest good" which, according to him, forms the final objective of the cultural subject, *i.e.* " reason ", plays on the one hand, the rôle of highest moral imperative (*Sollen*), in so far as it implies moral laws as its intrinsic prescriptions, but, on the other hand, it should belong to will (*Wollen*) so far as it constitutes the wholeness of the object of practical reason.[1] Kant even declares that freedom which lies under the notion of the highest good inheres in the correspondence of *Sollen* (moral imperative) and *Wollen* (will).[2] In other words, what is experienced as a moral imperative (*Sollen*) by the sense (=natural subject in our terms)

---

1) *Kritik der praktischen Vernunft.* S. 106 f.
2) In this respect, see my *"Philosophy of Religion,"* § 20, p. 111 ff. Kant, *Grundlegung zur Metaphysik der Sitten*, S. 449; S. 455.

is what is desired (*Wollen*) by the reason (=cultural subject). In short, no matter what kind of activity it may be, as long as it bears the character of the self-realization of the cultural subject, it is natural that, as manifestation of the subject or the original life itself which is always directed toward the effectuation of its being, it endeavors to accomplish itself. But the success of this effort depends not upon the subject itself, but upon its relationship with others. Others as potentiality or materials help the subject to act and achieve itself, but at the same time they work as impeding agents. As it is in natural life, otherness is an indestructible, necessary factor in cultural life. According to teleological belief, while this fact is taken into consideration in various forms and grades, still they maintain that the accomplishment of activity and attainment of the ultimate purpose of the subject can be effectuated under the condition that the subject may exist endlessly. Is this proposition really admissible?

As in the case of natural life, it is also the otherness which works as the source of temporal flux in cultural life. If otherness is perfectly identified with selfhood, and works as a faithful instrument for the achievement of the self, there will be found only pure present and both the future and the past will disappear. This is nothing but a state where all activities cease to function and in that sense here temporality may be completely overcome. But there is no possibility whatever that such a state may be realized. Cultural life requires others as its necessary condition. And in so far as it expects otherness, it must suffer from incessant obstruction or oppression coming from others. In natural life, this takes the form of the perpetual disappearance of the present into the past, or nothingness. Because cultural life is built on this basis, cultural time also presents an aspect of flux. There the present contains the past and the future as its intrinsic moments. Consequently the activity which basically characterizes the subject plays the rôle of linking the past and the future in or through the present. But this connection should be repeated moment after moment since it is a process with a moving center. This repetition is not only experienced by the cultural subject, but can be stabilized in a form or order of the objective world of reality. This is called objective time. Essentially it is a homogeneous continuity of the transient present. And as this continuity sees no end, endlessness is the intrinsic character of objective time. But even in teleological demonstration it is accepted as a fact that every present is in constant motion and every activity is ended in its incompleteness. Therefore, all the more, one tries to supplement the defect of the individual present and fragmentary activity by assuming their infinite continuity and one believes in its possibility. That is, endlessness which bears the title of the conqueror of temporality becomes one of the important factors for self-assertion and self-realization, which are the most essential character of the subject. Here a true or perfect life means an endless life.

But it has already been discussed many times from various standpoints that endlessness is not any conquering of temporality at all, but rather it is a prolongation or enlargement of temporality's intrinsic defect. Immortality or eternal life in the sense of endlessness is not any accomplishment of life at all; it is a continuity of imperfection or a thoroughgoing prolongation of non-perfection. For if it attains perfection, the endless continuity of being will become useless. It is because of something inherent in life and its activity, which has no room for realization, that the prolongation of endlessness is demanded. Where does this intrinsic defect come from? It comes from the relation with others. Now, to live means to live with others. In natural life, which is the basis of all the different stages of life as well as the source of all the degrees of temporality, fellowship with others is carried out in its immediacy. The subject which rushes straight ahead without looking about meets an existing other which rushes ahead in this same way. There life is disclosed simply in its self-assertion. And this blind self-assertion will, contrary to its original intention, be ended in its own destruction. As is often stated above, here lies the source of all the annoyances of temporality. In cultural life, that which comes into direct contact with it is an object and, as ideal being, it has no real center of existence in itself and stands on the side of the possible self for the subject. To that extent the pressure and intervention of others are alleviated and the annoyance of temporality mitigated. But here again the perfect disappearance of others means destruction of the subject as well. So that which allows the subject to realize itself is that which interferes with it. In this regard, the difficulty is just the same as in natural life, back to which its source should be traced. Therefore, unless the fellowship with others may take some other form, so that the subject may be liberated from the pressure and intrusion of others, one can never expect any overcoming of temporality.

## ( 6 )

Such transformation (*hen-kaku*, change and renovation) is brought about when both the subject and others develop completely new characters. But since in the actual life of this world, where natural life constantly forms the basic character of the subject, the subject has no power to change the basic relation with others, everything depends on the others. As will be discussed later, when life ascends from the stage of culture to that of religion, an other reveals itself in its concealed depth and thereby the subject changes itself entirely and thus the fellowship with the other will be shown in a new feature of a life with a person, and there, for the first time, temporality will be strictly and truly overcome and eternity will be realized. Of course, even at the stage of cultural life, as the nature of others is taken into consideration, there may be found some effort in this direction. Even though it may be unsuccessful in the long run, it is an earnest effort in the very nature of life for attaining eternity and should be taken into our consideration.

The first effort is already observable at the level of (false) eternity in the sense of immortality of the soul, *i.e.* endlessness which is the direct object of our present study. That is, to take a step further, at this level others or, in this case, the objective world of reality, are regarded as cooperating with the achievement of the selfhood of the subject, despite their otherness, and helping their activity without any interference. But in their actuality the really existing others do not necessarily cooperate with the subject; therefore, a certain kind or degree of transcendence is required. Thus a pure and true being in a higher dimension is established to come into direct fellowship with the actual subject. This is the standpoint of metaphysics which is distinguished from experimental sciences.[1] The systems of metaphysics are not simple and unitary. If we take extreme examples, there are ones which are more remarkable in their transcendence and the others which are not so. Striving for the separation from natural life and reality, the former try to go up to pure object or pure conceptual being and to attain the highest reality by ascribing an existing reality to it.[2] As the alienation from the objective world of reality, that is, from nature (in the broader sense), is maintained, so the cognition of the self is the sole and proper passage to it. This is metaphysics, *i.e.* idealistic metaphysics, in its strict sense. Different from this, the second type endeavors to push along the way which the cognition of the objective world of reality has taken. There the return from the world of objects to natural life or reality is admitted as such. Only the relation between the objects is led to the ultimate end and perfection. This is the kind of metaphysics to which we are now referring. Of course, as we have often stated, endlessness and imperfection are the essential characteristics of the

---

1) As to the descripiton which follows, see several passages of my *Philosophy of Religion*, especially, § 15 seq., § 27 seq. and § 45 seq.
2) See p. 26 seq. of this book.

objective world of reality. Therefore no metaphysics is possible, unless it seeks for a pure ideal being in some form and degree, that is, unless it gets the help of idealistic metaphysics. But this "realistic" metaphysics has a particular feature of directly relating the highest reality to the world of objective reality, that is, of advocating its immanence, to use the more popular term. In the category of the highest reality we may include cosmic order, cosmic reason or providence, etc. But as is mentioned above, because it implies a certain personification to ascribe reality to objects, these ideas may often be all-inclusive and integrated in the concept of "god", in which they may find their clear and perfect expression. In this case, the notion of god may correspond to the notion of the same name in religion, as far as it means an absolute reality, so that they may be identified in some sense, but here it is considered as a content of objective cognition. That is, god here is an all-inclusive cultural subject which expresses itself in the world of objective reality in such conceptual references as order, reason, providence, etc., realizing it and giving it an end. But still it is the other which is objectified and enlarged to the maximum. Thus the self-achievement of the god would inevitably lead the human subject to its perfection and completion. This view of the world is called theism and is widely accepted throughout the ages everywhere.[1] The first and a typical example is the concept of artificer (*demiourgos*) in Plato which is furnished with theoretical and academic reasoning. With the help or supposition of theism, the immortality and eternity of the human subject seem to have gained their solid basis.

But is such an all-inclusive, omnipotent, absolute reality actually needed for the cognition of the world of objective reality? Does cosmic relation or order indicate or allow any realization or end? Is metaphysics after all possible? We have neither time nor need of arguing this matter which was indeed one of the principal issues

---

1)   Concerning theism, see my *Philosophy of Religion*, §§ 27, 28; especially § 45.

in Kantian philosophy. We shall start from the fact that theism has long been existed as a faith and shall be contented by asking whether it can satisfy its *raison d'être* and whether it can carry out its duty. That is, what we must ask here is whether the theistic view of the world can promise perfect self-accomplishment or self-realization which is a demand coming from the heart of the human subject. Our answer is, of course, negative. Theism is one of the cosmic views. From the standpoint of contemplation, it tries to teach us what the cosmic order is and how the absolute subject which expresses itself in this order works. There the human subject should find satisfaction in being a sheer observer or by-stander. It is maintained that god always accomplishes its self-assertion and brings an end and completion to its own activity. Admitting this, we must say that it deals with some other objective being called god which has nothing to do with the human subject. It is not always clear that the human subject can participate in the fulfillment of the activity of god. As a matter of fact, it still lives in the midst of time and is exposed to the violence of death and destruction. That which the human subject may experience will be simply the activity of a self which never realizes itself. Let us take a step further and suppose that the human subject may be able to participate in the self-realization of the cosmic reality. Then it simply means that god expresses himself in cultural life in a certain limited period of time. But no matter whether that which expresses itself is a man or god, unless the essential character of life be changed or transformed, it is hopeless to solve the problem of temporality. And this will lead us to the final and most basic point. Despite the fact that the other, *i.e.* the god in this case, is objectified, magnified and garnished with several attributes and titles which signify excellence or eminence, so far as it is essentially a cultural subject, it should carry the same character and stand on the same ground in respect of its temporal character as human subject. Could we expect that such activity of the other delivers human activity from the incompleteness and fragmentariness which come from the very essence of man? Can even this other itself evade the miserable reality of the yoke of temporality? The answer is clearly " No!" Thus we are obliged to make up our mind here to leave the world of objective reality and its " false eternity."

# Chapter Six

# Non-temporality (Timelessness)

## ( 1 )

We still remain in the domain of cultural life. But we must leave activity behind. So what is left to us is contemplation. What we have described of contemplation and its reference to time can be summarized as follows:[1] Contemplation belongs also to the category of activity. But it endeavors to achieve the proper objective of cultural life by delivering from and surpassing the character of activity, while it is itself an activity. It means that by doing so, the subject will express itself completely and others will become its faithful instruments for the realization of selfhood. The objects exhaustively express the subject and the subject discloses itself to the last, so that there may be no traces of selfhood which acts or of otherness which is acted upon and the tension and instability between the two may be perfectly removed. Thus the objects completely develop their own particular character as conceptual beings which have no hidden centers of their own; whereas the subject reposes quietly and looks into the transparently clear shapes of the objects. That is contemplation. In contemplation the temporal aspect of cultural life is more deeply driven home. In cultural life the subject and its " present " dominate all the others and both the past and the future are comprehended in it as its formative factors. But such inner structure came into existence by the fact that in the aspect of objects two fields which represent selfhood and otherness, respectively, coexist although they are differentiated and activity comes into being as a relationship of

1) See pp. 23—32; 33—40 of this book.

the two. Then what does it mean to be delivered from the active character? It means the destruction of the inner structure which comprises the past and the future in it. In other words, the temporal aspect of contemplation is found simply in a pure present or a " now " which knows neither the past nor the future. There will be neither " was " nor " will be ", but simply " is ". The pure present or the pure being is an absolute being which internally and externally embraces no non-being.

This is the very notion of " eternity " which philosophy has dealt with for ages.[1] Although the term " eternity " does not appear, the principal thought is clearly expressed in the philosophy of Parmenides. Probably it was Plato who first used the word. Standing on the basis of those predecessors, Plotinus tried to define the concept more precisely. And his thought has dominated the entire field of philosophy since the middle ages through the hands of Proclus, Augustine, Boethius, Thomas Aquinas and others.[2] We can safely say without exaggeration that after Plotinus no really new thought on eternity has been developed up to now. But in so far as philosophy does not go beyond itself and try to attain a higher perspective on life and endeavors to remain peacefully in its position which represents the highest step of cultural life, it is a natural consequence that the concept of " eternity " is inevitably apprehended in such a manner. As is stated above, so far as the two kinds of images or fields which represent selfhood and otherness are related to each other, there still remains the character of activity and therefore, the very status which is requested by pure contemplation, i.e. by the very nature of contemplation, cannot be fully realized. It is the duty of philosophy to stand on the highest level of reflection, to alienate objective contents

1) Plato, *Timaeus*, 37D seqq. Plotinus, *Enneades*, III, 7, 3—5. Proclus, *Elementa theologiae*, 52 seqq. Augustinus, *Confessiones*, XI, 11 seqq. Boethius, *De consolatione philosophiae*, V, 6; *De Trinitate*, 4. Thomas Aquinas, *Summa theologiae*, I, 10.
2) About Martin Heidegger, an exceptional thinker, see my *Philosophy of Religion*, § 51, note 1.

based on selfhood and form from those based on otherness and matter, to grant the former their independence and transcendence and to stabilize them. It is philosophy which makes pure contemplation possible and by which pure forms and objects in a higher dimension come into being. When these highly pure objects are seen from the temporal perspective, they manifest the very characteristic of eternity in the sense of " non-temporality " (or timelessness, *Zeitlosigkeit*) .

The notion of timelessness is already found in the thought of Parmenides, but it was Plato who examined thoroughly the nature and significance of the being of the objects on the higher level which are super-temporal in nature. Plato gave a proper content to philosophy and made a really positive contribution to the understanding of eternity. Being in the world of objective reality is subjected to the rule of outwardness and relationship (or relativity) in general, and to spatiality and also to temporality in particular,[1] so that if we say, " Something is beautiful ", the reference is made simply *here, now, at this point, to this particular person,* and it comes into being to perish and obtains its being to lose. Quite different from this, ideas transcend outwardness and relationship, neither come into being nor perish and maintain their selfhood and selfsameness to the last. That is, they stay in their pure and simple beings and forms, *i.e.* true beings and forms, indeed they *are* themselves such beings and forms.[2] And eternity and immortality (ἀεὶ ὄν, ἀθάνατον, αἰών, αἰώνιον) are the characteristics of such pure beings at the highest level.[3] Plotinus basically succeeded this thought and arranged all these ideal beings into the world of oneness, *i.e.* world of

---

1) In this respect, see p. 43 seqq. of this book.
2) *Symposium*, 211A seqq.: *Phaedo*, 78C seqq.: 80B.
3) Also we find a term αἴδιον in *Timaeus* 37D. This is the very origin of the distinction of *aeternitas* (eternity) and *sempiternitas* (endlessness) which one can find in later thought (*e.g.* Boethius, *De Trinitate*, 4.) . But as Cornford pointed out (in his *Plato's Cosmology*, p. 98) , this distinction is not yet fully clear in Plato. In my opinion, the distinction of the two in Plotinus (III, 7, 5) is not quite the same, either.

thinking (κόσμος νοητός). Consequently he put special emphasis on the totality in defining the concept of eternity.[1] As we have seen it, when we think about the fragmentary, incomplete character of temporality, we should say that this explanation of the nature of pure objects is quite adequate. The totality immediately calls forth limitlessness (ἄ-πειρον).[2] And here appears the true limitlessness which means completeness (accomplishedness) in contrast to the false limitlessness of endlessness.

## (2)

There is no room for doubting that this "timelessness" is truly deliverance from temporality in the strict sense of the word. We have seen that endless time is rather a prolongation or extension of temporality than its overcoming. But now for the first time a realm of being which perfectly transcends temporality is developed before our very eyes. Quite unlike those existences which appear and disappear, which are carried away in the current of time, buried in the tomb of extermination or driven away to wander in the field of endless deception, here the motionless, imperishable beings are finally disclosed. Thereby liberation and freedom which are the intrinsic objectives of cultural life seem to have been perfectly achieved.

This, however, is too hasty a judgment. Are the beings which are considered timeless or super-temporal really capable of overcoming temporality? Pure forms, i.e. ideas, are the objects which are separated from otherness, and which signify pure selfhood. If such objects were to establish themselves, they would be the perfect self-expression of the subject and consequently their super-temporal character would, at the same time, mean and ascertain the super-temporal character

---

1) The definition of the concepts *totum praesens* (Augustinus) and *totum simul* (Boethius and Thomas Aquinas) comes from this source. Here we can already find such phrases as ἀεὶ πάρον τὸ πάν or ἅμα τὰ πάντα (III, 7, 3) etc.
2) Plotinus, III, 7, 5.

of the subject itself. Is this really possible? Here we must recall the dual characteristics of contemplation.[1] Contemplation is a kind of activity. In agreeing that objects are intrinsically conceptual beings, the subject expresses itself in them and tries to hide and enjoy serenity in the shade of the objects as disclosed self. Nevertheless in so far as contemplation is a contemplating act which consists of a fellowship of what is contemplated and what contemplates, the objects belong to the category of others and however much closer the distance may become, they stand against the subject at a certain distance. So far contemplation will not attain its aim and the trait of activity still remains. This means that temporality remains unconquered. Then what does the conquering of activity and temporality really mean and by what measure can we attain it? It means the conquering of otherness, and we may be able to attain it thereby. Thus first the otherness in the aspect of objects will gradually be weakened and the link between objects will become much closer. The link itself is an expression of the selfhood of the subject and it is rooted in and signifies the identity of the latter, so that the closer linkage should also take a form of the homogenization of the content. Philosophy which is intensively guided by the laws of logic inevitably reaches the notion of the one (τὸ ἕν, according to Plotinus' term) which has conquered all others and otherness. The notion of totality or limitlessness inevitably develops into the concept of monism (oneness). But this overcoming, in reverse, simply implies the destruction of the self in reality. The objects which are absorbed in the one point are something contentless, unrelated and meaningless, and cannot fulfil their office of expression and be the objects of contemplation. Thus all being will sink into non-being and all light will be covered by darkness. Secondly, the overcoming of otherness existing between the subject and objects tempts us to the same danger. The subject which has lost others in which it

1) As to the following discussion, see pp. 20—32 of this book.

had expressed itself loses its selfhood and, after all, is reduced to naught. Just as objects which became the possession of the subject are no longer objects, so the subject which has completely expressed itself and become disclosed loses its really existing character as a hidden center, and disappears into hallucination. The philosophy of contemplation inevitably brings about perfect unity of the subject and object, but this unity may be nothing other than the abolition of the self by its complete effectuation. Temporality may be resolved by the negation of otherness, but it may mean only an extermination of the self in the subject. The permanent now (*nunc permanens*) which should overcome the flowing now (*nunc currens*) is simply a forfeiture of all the " nows ".[1]

Consequently the subject should still remain active. But in activity both otherness and selfhood constitute its necessary conditions. What is more fundamental is the otherness of objects. The otherness which is essentially furnished in the nature of objects is expressed as otherness in their mutual relationship. A link which is an expression of the selfhood comes into being only as a relation between one and others, that is, more precisely, between the aspect or field which represents selfhood and that which represents otherness, or between what acts and what is acted upon; but all these come from the otherness proper to the nature of objects. Going further back to the original source, we must reach the otherness of really existing being, but that is not our question for the moment. Now contemplation as an activity tries to overcome this otherness and bring its selfhood to perfection. Objectively, it takes the form of belittling material things and attaching importance to formal things. More particularly, the relation is emphasized and the content which represents selfhood and activity becomes purer and more influential. For example, causal relation becomes logical, cause comes to be a

---

1) Boethius, *De Trinitate.* 4. Since the Middle Ages, "staying now" or "*nunc stans*" was employed as a term expressing the super-temporal aspect in philosophy.

ground and finally all becomes or is resolved into principle and thus unity or totality gradually embraces and absorbs in itself all differences and particularity. Philosophy tries to effectuate this tendency to the end. This is her duty. As far as she does not fall into the insanity of believing she is omnipotent and of not acknowledging any being except that of pure objects (if there be any such idea in effect, it should be called literally insane), philosophy must differentiate and classify the beings in the objective world in order to satisfy her intension. The Platonic theory of the two kinds of being (δύο εἴδη τῶν ὄντων) is the most original and typical example which had a great influence upon subsequent philosophy. But it is only possible if the act of reflection be effectuated more deeply in the course of the development of natural life into cultural life and the content which implies selfhood or formality be separated, isolated and stabilized as something independent and transcendent. Therefore, from the point of view of the totality of cultural life, philosophy is an act of just abstracting the aspect of the self-achievement of the subject, of concentrating entirely her attention on it, forgetting all other aspects. The aspect of selfhood which is abstracted is what gives life its form and determines its character. That is, it is the true aspect of its being, its true being, its essence—what is called by Plato ὄντως ὄν or οὐσία. Consequently by concentrating our effort on contemplating and understanding it, we can attain a higher or deeper apprehension of life itself.[1] But we must not forget that this is simply an effective and appropriate means of reaching a certain objective and

---

[1] Rf. Lotze, *Logik*. Drittes Buch, 2tes Kapitel. (Phil. Bibl. S. 510 ff.) Lotze distinguishes the mode of being of the Idea, in its strict sense (*i.e. Sein* or *Wirklichkeit*) from *Gelten* (to be valid or applicable) and criticized Plato for confusing the two. As far as it is a criticism of the metaphysical development of the theory of Ideas in Plato and an effort to be true to the most pure and basic motive and character of philosophy of idealism, this interpretation is right. From the standpoint of the philosophy of value Windelband put at the center of his thought this distinction between *Sein* and *Gelten*. His interpretation of eternity (see "*Sub specie aeternitatis*" in his *Präludien*) is an excellent work of unique importance, in so far as it does not take the road of metaphysics and accepts frankly the temporality of the subject.

91

what is done here is to remove unnecessary obstacles from our eyes, to forget them for the moment. Those who wish to enter the world of pure form or essence should abandon and forget all the determinations which may suggest activity and temporality. As is the case with all areas of science, to a certain degree philosophy is an especially excellent "technique for forgetting" in its perfect sense. To be faithful to her duty, she should forget her home—time and temporality —or even close her eyes to the destiny of the death of the subject itself. But to forget or not to see it does not at all mean either to efface it or to overcome it. The temporality of the subject still continues to exist and exercise its terror. When one who has been absorbed in contemplation of eternal truth, "forgetful of himself", "comes back to himself," can he not realize that he is being carried away in the flux of time and forced to be drowned in it?

( 3 )

Although it may bring some joy and security, all the efforts to alienate temporality from our horizon is after all a momentary consolation. In so far as objects are to be taken into the subject as its material factors for the achievement of the self and to be abandoned to its disposal, there will be no hope of overcoming temporality. There will be only one way left. The independence and otherness of objects should be emphasized. As we have seen,[1] in the case of the world of objective reality the same way was to be followed. There objects are attributed to real others or naturally existing being. But in pure beings, this road is entirely closed from the outset. From the start, coming back to natural reality has been refused to the pure objects of the highest level, which overcame it through the two steps of reflection. There remains for philosophy only to give reality to ideal beings and to install them directly on the throne of the highest reality. This is

---

1)  Rf. p. 26 and p. 43 seqq. of this book..

"metaphysics."[1] As we have mentioned above, there are two types of metaphysics. The metaphysics of immanence tries to reduce objective cognition to its principle and the objective world of reality further to the basic reality from which it gained its being. But this is only possible by transcendence which is achieved by the objects at the highest level. Therefore, the metaphysics of immanence acquires its title of metaphysics by virtue of the metaphysics of transcendence. Therefore it is not an exaggeration to say that there is no metaphysics other than that of idealism. Ideal beings in their pure essence perfectly disclose themselves and possesses no hidden center or no center as a reality which may refuse to allow others to trespass on them. So it is basically not possible to install them directly on the seat of reality. Nevertheless since Plato many great thinkers have made their way onto this forbidden path. It teaches us that life comes into being only through a fellowship with reality and the longing for that reality is rooted in the depth of human nature. In short, a desire to have contentment in an ultimate reality is properly religious.[2] Here we cannot go into detail, but it may be said that, as this aspiration is satisfied not by the metaphysical philosophy of idealism, but simply by the religion of the love of personalism, so the longing for eternity will never be satisfied in this stage.

As is already stated regarding the theistic view of the world,[3] so far as the highest reality is the proper object of contemplation, it is quite doubtful whether and how its super-temporal character may be able to serve in resolving the temporality of the human subject. Is there any contradiction between the fact that the cognition of the highest reality is free from temporal restriction and the fact that the cognizing subject is submitted to that restriction? What will happen if we suppose that the highest reality comes into fellowship with the world of temporality and lifts the human subject up into the higher

1) Rf. p. 26, p. 80 seqq. of this book.
2) Rf. my *Philosophy of Religion*, § 15 seq.
3) Rf. p. 80 seq. of this book.

world? The greatest difficulty for the metaphysics of idealism is to find a link between the eternal and the temporal. From Plato to Spinoza and Hegel, all the thinkers who held a dualistic view took a false step in this problem.[1] Of course, they tried to find an answer to the matter, too. But simply to talk about the link and to put it in an intelligible form are not identical. Indeed, even if we could solve the problem by establishing a link as true, the link as well as the temporality which forms one end of it would leave temporal being and find a new home in the world of eternity as a timeless super-temporal object, but, nevertheless, what is temporal would continue to maintain the same inconstant being. The fact that the concept of temporality is super-temporal has nothing to do with the fact that the temporal being remains temporal. Highest reality here means an objective, conceptual being that is elevated into the seat of reality as it is. So it is deprived of selfhood. It is deprived of the activity of working upon temporal beings. Although ideas, forms or categories such as force, activity, development, cause, subject, substance and so on may imply their noble and brilliant beings which are to be observed in the serene world of eternity, the perishable, temporal world in which we are living will not be in the slightest influenced by them. When we take the highest reality—or god in ordinary usage—for a highest and absolute subject which acts directly upon the objective world of reality, we must return to the so-called theism that we have already commented upon in the cosmic view of the philosophy of immanence. Then, how can this reality which works in the middle of the temporal world be freed from temporality and keep its super-temporal character? This will be the immediate refutation which may arise from the opposite camp.

---

1) Rf. my *Study of Spinoza*. Hegel tried to answer this in his dialectics. But all the references and development which were taught by him are simply events in the world of ideas. When he says: "the rational is the real and the real is the rational", his term "real" or "actual" is nothing but the ὄντως ὄν of Plato.

(4)

The idea that the human subject will become super-temporal through unity, fellowship or communion with another super-temporal reality—god—by means of contemplation or intuition is quite common in various religions and philosophies throughout the ages. Mysticism in its pure and strict sense is a thoroughgoing attempt in this direction. Even in the philosophies which do not try to go so far as to say that man and god may be perfectly one but which simply show some mystic tendency or trend, when attention was given to the problem of eternity, in most of the cases the eternity not only of the object is usually advocated, but also the eternity of the human subject. One of the leading thoughts of the Hellenistic period which is colored by the most vivid spirit of the classical period in the history of religion was: "To become god by seeing him."[1] Among philosophers we can indicate the names of Plato, Spinoza, Fichte and others as examples.[2] The famous word of Schleiermacher: "To become one with the unlimited in the midst of limitedness and to be eternal in an instant—this is immortality in religion," is simply a succinct and impressive expression of a similar thought.[3]

Where does such a thought originate? It comes, of course, from the very nature of contemplation. In contemplation what the subject

---

1) This thought is expressed in the Bible (*Corinthian* II, 3, 18). Also see Bousset, *Kyrios Christos,* p. 197 seq. (Under the title of "Vergottung durch Gottesschau"); Reitzenstein, *Die hellenistischen Mysterienreligionen.* p. 357 f. J. Weiss, *Urchristentum,* p. 406.

2) In *Theaetetus,* 176B, it is indicated that "to be like god" is one of the merits of philosophy. As to the theory of immortality of the soul in *Phaedon,* see the following chapter; Plotinus, IV, 7, 10; III, 7, 5; Also see Spinoza's theories of *scientia intuitiva* and *amor dei intellectualis;* Fichte, *Anweisung zum seligen Leben,* V. 487 seq.; *Grundzüge des gegenwärtigen Zeitalters,* VII, 235 seq. (Here it is especially clearly expressed.) In Hegel, the subject enters into the world of eternity to reside there, but it is only as an idea of the selfhood of the subject, *i.e.* as a pure object. His idealism is most thoroughgoing.

3) *Reden über die Religion,*[1] p. 133. Such an eternity of the subject can be achieved by *Anschauen des Universums.*

95

faces is the object as ideal being. The subject whose active character is undiscovered stands before the transparent form of the disclosed self. An object which has no center of reality of its own and has neither depth nor profundity is a plane being. It achieves its proper mission by entering into perfect unity with the subject by overcoming all the distances and obscurities. And the essential character of such an object is timelessness. This is a matter neither of inference nor of conviction which we see in the case of immortality and (false) eternity coming from the endlessness of objective time; it is something that should be experienced directly now as the essential nature of object. Moreover, whereas endlessness implied incessant inachievement and continual dissatisfaction, here the subject can repose in the pure present without any past nor future and enjoy a happy life of perfection. And this life is accomplished only in its unity with the object. It is not without reason that in the contemplation of timeless being, the subject can experience its super-temporal being. It is, however, a sheer feeling or sentiment. What is really experienced is merely the timelessness of the object. If the highest reality is truly a reality, the subject can never anticipate direct unity with it. As far as the subject safeguards its own center and the super-temporal being refuses penetration by others, both—especially the subject in this case—are, from the beginning, unable to go beyond some external contact. Therefore, if the super-temporal being permits any unity with it, it will be only in its capacity of ideal being. So the problem is carried backward. It is needless to reiterate that ideal being can neither bring forth nor safeguard the super-temporal character of the subject.

But there is still left one way to follow. That is to say, we must start from the original source of our experience and apprehend its conditions so that we may be able to set the cause or fact which makes our experience possible by virtue of inference. The fact that the subject of contemplation experiences the object as something close, intimate or homogeneous proves that the two are identical in their being, in their essence, or, in some cases, even in their existence, although they retain their respective beings. Only those which are originally identical can achieve unity. It is because the subject is itself super-temporal that it can cognize or even become one with super-temporal objects... It is, however, quite obvious that this thought derives from the point of view that cultural life is something ultimate. Strictly speaking, in this stage there is nothing but the present and being. What *is* at this moment should come from what *is*, and what is identical should come from what is identical. Accordingly, one can find here neither death nor nothingness in their strict senses. So nothing can be created out of nothingness. That is, there is no room for creation. In the field of religion mysticism clearly manifests such a tendency. In the realm of philosophy or metaphysics, the so-called pantheistic view of the world is based on it. This kind of thinking, however, has a strong influence in all the different fields of philosophy. In our present subject-matter we also notice the same development of this basic thought.

It should be regarded as quite natural that the philosophy that congition is a conjoining or unity of something homogenous or identical prevailed very widely among the ancient Greeks who were the pioneers of cultural philosophy or idealism in the history of the world. It would not be a prejudice to say that the obvious exception was Anaxagoras. Although it was quite primitive in form, the thought was expressed by Empedocles who said, " One sees earth with earth and water with water."[1]  According to Aristotle,[2] cognition takes place in the form of the unity of subject and object.

An actualized cognition is identical with its object. The primary objective of reason is to become one with the cognized object and, as

1) Fr. 109. γαίῃ μὲν γὰρ γαῖαν ὀπώπαμεν, ὕδατι δ' ὕδωρ,
2) See my *Philosophy of Religion*, § 26. The Aristotelean theory that poten-tiality after all derives from actuality is based on the principle of culturalism which we have already examined in this book. A part of the theory of νοῦς ποιητικός should also be understood from this side. "Being" always precedes "becoming".

97

everything can be the object of cognition, with being in general. But for that, before any cognition may take place, it is required that there be identity of subject and object either potentially (in the case of human cognition) or actually (in the so-called active intellect which is a dynamic power of actualizing potentiality) ... Plotinus expressed the same thought in his poetical phrasing: " Only the eyes which have become like the sun can see it and the soul which has become beautiful can sense beauty."[1] According to him, the soul becomes eternal and divine by contemplating something eternal and divine and thus goes back to its forgotten birthplace. Spinoza maintains that the cognition which means unity of object and subject presupposes identity or unity of substance (substantia). The immortality of a human being comes from his intuitive knowledge of god and the intellectual love toward god which results immediately and inevitably from that knowledge. His immortality is based upon the fact that he himself possesses the eternal mode (aeternus modus) of god. Therefore, the love of man toward god, or eternity, is the equivalent of the self-love of god.

When we reconsider the thought which is derived from the spirit of cultural philosophy in relation to the self-assertiveness which characterizes cultural life, we shall immediately discover the following situation: wherever the subject expresses itselft, there are being, identity, and the present. They all derive from the selfhood of the subject. But the selfhood can gain reality only through the activity of its self-assertion. If the subject were super-temporal in reality from the beginning, there would be no ambiguity, but in fact, such a subject may simply be one which is put in the form of a pure object, i.e. the idea or the essence of the subject. So it would be self-evident that it is timeless or super-temporal, but at the price of ceasing to be a subject in reality. The νοῦς of Aristotle and Plotinus, the *Geist* (mind) of Hegel and others are the typical examples of such a subject. They

---

1)   I, 6, 9.   This is the source of the famous saying of Goethe.

remain in a form of super-temporal self-contemplation (νόησις νοήσεως in Aristotelean terminology) and are super-temporal both as objects and subjects. But as has been said, such super-temporality or timelessness as an object of sheer contemplation means simply a picture cake to the actual subject who is suffering in the yoke of temporality. If the subject is basically identical or homogeneous with its object, and consequently is equally super-temporal, this self or its essence should be actualized in a form of reality. But this requires an activity of the subject, namely its temporality. Therefore, if we seek for eternity or immortality, what we gain may be nothing but endless temporality. In so far as it clearly exposes this situation, Plato's demonstration of the immortality of the soul attracts our attention.[1] Standing on the ground of a pure and simple idealism he taught two kinds of being. The one is invisible and pure, without any earthly vices, simple in form, always identical in itself, eternal, immortal and divine. The other has all the opposite characteristics. The soul belongs to the second, the category of earthly being. But as it also belongs to the same genus as eternal being, it ascends into heaven up to the home of immortal, changeless beings, remains there for ever and, thanks to fellowship with them, it escapes the fate of the earthly wanderer and maintains its ever-identical being and so on... We are deeply impressed by the confession of an example of the experience of this pure and true idealist. But what Plato reckoned as immortality of the soul was not at all a development of the soul or fellowship with the eternal being such as would be attained at the center of our life at any moment. It was rather an endless being which would be realized after our death. The foregoing argument was adduced simply as one of the grounds by which he thought he could prove immortality of the soul in this sense. Then why is it not allowed to us to obtain eternal life even here in this world? Because the soul shares its life with the body so that we cannot lead a life of pure contemplation. That is, unless its perfect

1)  *Phaedon*, 79 D.

unity with pure contemplation or eternity were real from the outset as an established fact, exercise (μελέτη) will be needed. But alas its fruit is obtained only after our death.[1] But would not the exercise be a temporal activity? When one says that the objective can be achieved after death, is that not different from a simple confession of the impossibility of attaining that objective, if one sees it from a purely idealistic standpoint? While the human subject seeks for a deliverance from this world or salvation by his own power either by becoming himself the highest being or eternity or by being himself divine and super-temporal, will he not find himself only in a state of hopelessness or despair?

---

1) Contrary to the description of the experience of pure object which is extremely clear, his demonstration of the immortality of the soul which is based upon it is very ambiguous and almost chaotic. If death is a separation of the soul and body, the simple fact of death would signify a deliverance or liberation. But then philosophy is described as an exercise of death. But the death which is mentioned here does not mean the simple fact of death but liberation which may be granted after death only to those who have achieved philosophical training. It is called death only allegorically. That is, those who devote themselves to philosophical training can harvest the crop of the exercise. But would this exercise be continued after death as Kant and other modern thinkers have taught? The idea of immortality of the soul may require it, but Plato restricted this exercise to a certain period of time, as he taught it in his eschatology which shows some influence of Orphic religion. But we see a more fundamental contradiction in the fact that he required the exercise. If the soul were in itself super-temporal, why would such an exercise be needed? Even Plato himself was not theoretically contented with this demonstration. After all he gave up this theory and shifted into the next (and the last) stage of demonstration. In short, for him true eternity of life can only come into being in the contemplation of the eternal being which may be and should be realized whenever and wherever it may be; but since he could not put absolute confidence in such transitory sentiment or ecstasy in the mystic thinkers and since he possessed the kind of spirit which had to follow a more certain way, clearly realizing that the actual life of the subject is activity and self-realization, he finally fell into this chaotic confusion.

# Chapter Seven

# Eternity and Love

## 1. *Eros* and *Agape*

### ( 1 )

Already in the cultural life we have observed that there is some tendency toward surpassing and overcoming temporality. Indeed, we can even call it the most essential characteristic of the cultural life. Now for us, human beings, " to be " is " to live," and " to live " is " to assert ourselves." But on the other hand, it is a life directed toward others and comes into being only in the form of fellowship with an other. In the basic life which carries the whole structure of human existence, an other which stands against the subject exists *in reality* and the link with it is characterized by immediacy. Temporality is the essential feature of this natural life. Therefore, the overcoming of temporality should be the overcoming of this natural state of life. The problem lies in the relationship between the other in fellowship with the subject and its temporality, and the way they are related to each other. In accordance with the two (natural life and other) , the nature of the subject itself is also determined. In cultural life as it continues to assert itself, retaining its direct aspect, the subject attempts to develop and free itself and to deliver itself from temporality simply by changing the character of the other. In philosophy which mounts the summit of this path, even fellowship with others, *i.e.* pure forms and pure objects which are granted timelessness, seems to have been realized and the attempt at deliverance seems to achieve its aim. Nevertheless, all these endeavors end in failure. In cultural life, the other as possible self has neither a center of its own nor reality, and serves essentially as a factor in the realization of the subject. But as far as fellowship with natural life or real others is concerned, which are the basic source of the existence of the subject and the temporal flux which flows out of it, cultural life had no other recourse than to remain an idle spectator and give itself to the flux. Therefore, temporality could be overcome only when, in the place of its partial repair, life actually effects some fundamental, total transformation of its being. That is, when the subject comes into a completely new fellowship with an other, and both the other and the subject assume entirely new phases, we can expect the coming of eternity. " Love " is the very mode of life which is completely re-created in this manner. So we must go beyond the boundary of culture and proceed to the realm of religion.[1]

( 2 )

Love is fellowship of the subject with others. Since the subject asserts itself in life, love implies an effort and act of forming or keeping the fellowship. The fellowship is a relationship of life and does not allow any halt or standstill. Nor is it a simple contact or encounter, which by nature are indifferent to it or even work against it. On the contrary, fellowship is possible only as a unity or harmony.

This fellowship is the necessary basis for the actual life of a human being. What we call a human (or moral) relation is, in most cases, either this kind of fellowship of love or something built only on its basis. We cannot live even an instant without having unity and harmony with others. The more complicated the structure of our actual life, the more the variety of fellowship is found there. But after all, the variety may be reduced to the single relationship of love. This is evident in reality, but it will be explained more in particular through a theoretical analysis of the essence of life.

1) Concerning the following discussion, see my *Philosophy of Religion*, § 37 seq.

The essence of the subject as such lies in the fact that it forms the center of activity, that is, that it maintains, accomplishes, develops and expands its being. In short, the essence of the subject lies in its self-assertiveness. In other words, it should be found in the existence of its being. But this involves the existence of another party against which the subject asserts itself. That is, the subject essentially lives or exists toward others. This is clearly envisaged in our daily experience. Basically we exist face to face with other men. But often we also find ourselves in front of other things. At any rate, our existence is directed toward some other beings. When we want to go forward, we do so toward a something, and when we try to expand ourselves, we do so toward a somewhere. From this actual situation we are able to construct an abstract image of a power of exteriorization toward others. But if we believe that such a power exists as such—that is, that the true nature of the subject is to be found in such a power which goes forward and expands aimlessly into a sheer vacuum, we may be like those who sell an imaginary product for a real one. We must remember that such an idea of an absolute subject which has no partner, no relation whatever with others, may be established without contradiction in itself only when there is *a* subject—or *a* being *qua* objective other—which represents, acknowledges and maintains it as an objective situation or truth. The subject, that is, an existence, has twin aspects: on the one hand, it takes the form of self-assertion, but on the other, it is related to others, or it can establish its being only as a life toward others.—Here lies the most fundamental problem of life. And from there arises also the question of temporality and eternity.

Now from what we have viewed above, let us proceed to our observation into the characteristics of life of different levels in the light of love and fellowship. It is natural life which lies at the base of all and bears all forms of life as their foundation. It establishes itself in the direct relationship between the subject and the real others. So far as there is a linkage and contact with others, there must be something which is coexistent with them. In fact the subject never exists all by itself apart from others. Naturally it should be said that there is a relation somewhat similar to fellowship in natural life, too. If we recall that natural life lies at the basis of all the levels of life, we may safely say that this relation forms the basis of all the fellowships. But if we see it from the other side, we should say that this relation is the very destructive cause of all the fellowships. For the subject which enters into fellowship with others in its immediacy and which asserts itself without hesitation toward them, they mean nothing other than obstacles and resistances. Consequently, the achievement of the self-assertiveness unavoidably means the annihilation of others. In reverse, in so far as others exist persistently as such,—and their existence is also a *sine qua non* for that of the subject—the fellowship with others is a pressure and intervention on the subject and a forfeiture of its own existence. Therefore, even when it does not go to such an extent, the direct link of the subject with others in natural life is purely and simply external and outward. There we have seen the basic spatiality.[1] And it is the most typical and fundamental of all the relationships of the self and others which are excluding each other. There is no way of finding any fellowship, harmony or unity of the subject and others at that level. On the contrary, the destiny of natural life in its strict sense will be a cessation and annihilation of that very fellowship. The double aspect of the nature of the subject is disclosed here in a form of extremely undisguised self-contradiction. Moreover, its temporality, defects and contradictions all originate therein. The present (subject) which maintains its being by the link with the future (others) is driven away into the past or non-being by the same relationship. Being is always reduced to nothingness; that which comes into being always passes away and everything follows the endless road of perishing, tempted by temporal flux. So the overcoming of temporality should be a deliverance of natural life from this self-contradiction.

---

1) See p. 47 seq.

This is the very objective of cultural life.  As we have already mentioned, the essential character of cultural life lies in the fact that the subject which is delivered from the direct link with real others and freed from the peril of self-destruction coming from it, endeavors to assert itself to the end in a realm of freedom.  Now it tries to interpose something between its subject and itself, to avoid direct encountering and thus to establish co-existence and fellowship.  The object is such an intermediary agent.  But those which play the rôle of mediators of the fellowship vary according to the difference of the forms or levels of the fellowship.  Aristotle[1] called such a mediator τὸ φιλῆτον (that which is to be loved) and enumerated " the good ", " the delightful " and " the useful " as examples.  But we should not restrict it to these concepts of universal value.  Particular, steady human (or moral) relation or its special quality and further some elastic relations such as " neighbor " or its opposite, " man at a distance " (the man of future generations) [2] as well as various kinds of ideology, law and ideal—all these are to be called φιλῆτον.  They are the conditions and causes of the formation and maintenance of fellowship and thus specify its various types and contents.  We must specially emphasize the fact that this fellowship is achieved only by the mediation of these conditions and specifications, so they are the direct objects of fellowship and not the really existing others which are to be mediated by them. If we see love from the side of the attitude of the subject, we call it something which does not want to exist without others or which defines itself or asserts its being as something which is defined by others, but in that case the other which comes before it directly is always itself the mediator.  By giving up immediacy, but at the same time by entering into a new immediate relationship, we are able to attain fellowship and love.  If we call such a fellowship ἔρως, employing the terminology

1) *Ethica Nicomachea,* VIII, 1155 b.
2) Nietzsche, who refused "neighor-love" (*Nächstenliebe*) taught the "love at a distance" (*Fernstenliebe,* creative love of living in the future.)  See *Also Sprach Zarathustra,* I Teil: *"Von der Nächstenliebe."*

of Plato, we must say that it is the very love which can be attained at the level of—and only at the level of—cultural life.

## ( 3 )

It goes without saying that fellowship or unity can never be found between those who are completely separated or isolated. The subject is connected with others by some link or relationship. And for that a direct contact is necessary. Indirectness or mediation is established only on the basis of directness. In natural life everything is characterized by directness. As a consequence a real being collides with another being and thus both of them are destined to proceed along the way of self-destruction. The duty of cultural life is to reduce the danger of collision and to establish unity and harmony by posing an intermediary agent, that is, by entering into a new direct fellowship with others. If this is true, it is necessary to examine further the natures of these others and the linkage with them. As is clearly explained above, such intermediary agents cannot be otherwise than others as objects. But the mode of being of objects is conceptual. For the subject, such kinds of others are those in and through which it asserts itself, that is, factors of its self-realization. Objective others are essentially put under the influence of the subject and stand in especially closer relationship with it. They are essentially potential selfhood. The subject (*ego*) achieves its subjective character by absorbing objects into it and changing them into its own possession, indeed into itself. As otherness is absorbed into selfhood, both collision and conflict between the subject and others are taken away and unity and fellowship come into being. Thus love as *eros* is established by the enlargement of selfhood. It finds itself in any objects. Others are always the second self.[1] In love the subject will know that its own life or its own self will step out from a near, narrow and small circle, extend and

---

1) Ἐτσὶ γὰρ ὁ φίλος ἄλλος αὐτός—Aristotle, *Eth. Nic.* 1166a.

develop itself without fearing what is far, wide and great, so that finally it may be able to embrace under its wings the entire world, being in its wholeness. Thus the basic spatiality, that is, the outwardness which separates the self and others, seems to be completely annulled. But then how about its temporality? It is needless to repeat that the subject of cultural life, the *ego,* always lives in the present. Its temporal character is of the present. There the present involves in it both the past and the future simply as its contents or parts. Therefore, strictly speaking, for *eros* there exists only the present. Both the past and future of those which are loved call for our concern as if they were present right now. No matter how great the distance of time may be in the past or in the future, that does not reject the arising emotion of love. The happiness of love knows nothing to be added or nothing to be subtracted. Love always possesses everything. When one is filled with the ecstasy of love, a single instant may become a perfect eternity.

But from what we have dealt with in cultural temporality it is already clear that this is nothing but a castle in the air. The omnipotent present which props all being is, in fact, a present which is incessantly perishing. In so far as cultural life stands on the basis of natural life, love will also be determined by the character of natural life. The dual character of the nature of the subject which was discovered in natural life comes into cultural life under some disguised form and eats up the root of life until it finally falls by self-contradiction. Love as the self-realization of the subject should also have the nature of activity.[1] But it is based upon a necessary parallelism of selfhood and otherness as well as the unavoidable tension of the two. For objects it is essential to be others against the subject, but, having reference and function of the realization or expression of the subject, it is similarly essential to belong to the selfness of the subject. A thorough-going effectuation of one of the two may cause the destruction

1) As to activity, see p. 20 ff.

of life. If only otherness is asserted, life will be obliged to go back to the directness of nature. There fellowship will completely disappear. On the contrary, if only selfhood is asserted, the subject who exhausts itself in its realization will lose the center of life and by draining the source of life, in other words, by completely swallowing others and having no partner upon which it acts, it will dig the hole for its own grave. It is the discord between selfhood and otherness that makes life active, but it forces that very life to flow and change incessantly and stay always in an unfinished fragmentariness. Corresponding to this, fellowship as *eros* will always be fragmentary and unstable. Love gains its most satisfactory form as it reaches others and owns them. But here to gain it is to lose it and contentment quickly shifts into dissatisfaction. As Plato taught in his allegory, *Eros* is a half-breed who was born from *Penia* (the Poor) as she tried to get rid of her misery and misbehaved with *Poros* (the Rich).[1] Love is essentially an aspiration for or adoration of others.

Although in love one refers to eternity and even swears that his love will never change, at the level of cultural life, in so far as it stands under the influence of human nature, one can never break the bond of temporality. In love the subject looks for fellowship with an other, but once this fellowship is achieved and the other is taken into the self, it loses this fellowship and has to look for another. The existence of an other is an absolute condition for the establishment of fellowship. And this kind of other is found only in real others. This indicates what an important rôle natural life plays as a substructure of cultural life. But owing to its double character this natural life leads all activity including that of love into self-contradiction and makes it groan under the fetters of temporality. Therefore, in order to overcome temporality and enter into eternity, one must first be delivered from natural life as such and, at the same time, from the active character of life. And this means an establishment of firm fellowship of life bet-

1) *Symp.* 203.

ween the subject and others. When both of them cease to destroy each other's existence by collision or intrusion and a perfect unity and accord is established between them, all the uneasiness, incompleteness and fragmentariness of life will disappear as a matter of course and eternity will disclose itself in its plenitude.

It has long been the task of philosophy and religion to carry out this objective. We have already spent considerable space on eternity in the field of philosophy, that is, on timelessness. Although it is a kind of activity, contemplation aims at the overcoming of the active character or, more fundamentally speaking, the deliverance from the power of natural life. Therefore, its goal should be set in such a place where objects as others sever their link with natural reality and secure their own free, independent and autonomous being. Philosophy deals with such pure objects. Pure objects are free from all temporal restriction, transcend any distinction of the past, the present and the future and remain in ever-changeless self-identical being. It is this timeless, super-temporal being that philosophy names eternity. We need not repeat these points any more in detail. In such a pure contemplation, the subject stands in a very close relationship with its objects (*i.e.* others). All the irregularity on the surface of objects and the tension between selfhood and otherness which were found in activity are now taken away and there remains only otherness which is needed for the establishment of objects as such. Therefore the unity and harmony which can be found between the subject (self) and the others are of the highest degree. Accordingly, in this stage the relation of the subject and object which can be achieved in or by philosophy should be the most excellent and highest grade of love. According to history, since Plato gave it the name of *eros* in its best sense, many thinkers like Aristotle and Plotinus who have been under the influence of his philosophy taught in some sense or other the identity or the close relationship of the intuition and love, especially, of (or toward) god. Even in the *caritas* (love) of Augustine, who left a very deep influence on subsequent philosophy, although its relation to the intuition of God is somewhat ambiguously interpreted, as if it were the preliminary step of that intuition or as if the love implied the intuition, it is irrefutable that their link was very close.[1] Also the *amor dei intellectualis* (intellectual love of God) of Spinoza should be named as one of the most distinguished examples.

As pure contemplation in philosophy aims at perfect deliverance from natural life and is the principal characteristic of cultural life, so the love of truth as pure object which is the principal nature of philosophy is a perfect manifestation of cultural *eros*. *Eros* takes conceptual being as an intermediary of its fellowship with real objects. Such intermediary agents are the others which stand in a direct contact with the subject. Were we to suppose that all the linkages with natural life are severed, all the basic supports taken away and the independence of the agents of the direct linkage established and maintained to an end, there would appear simply the *eros* which forms fellowship with pure object. The deliverance from temporality would require such a leap or transcendence. In this respect, Plato has left us a very suggestive example (in his " *Symposium* "). Love first directs itself toward natural reality, *i.e.* man or thing, especially toward man. Thereby the intermediary agent is " the beautiful". But love toward a beautiful object. The deliverance from temporality would require such a leap It is the final target of *eros* to enter into eternity and immortality as it achieves itself in the good or in some value. There the beautiful which is the good in superior grade governs and embraces in it all the values. But so long as love directs itself toward natural reality, immortality ( = eternity) may be replaced by such substitutes as the

1) Rf. the two following books: Holl, *Gesammelte Schriften*, III, S. 81 ff. A. Nygren, *Eros und Agape*, II, S. 321 ff. Among the views of the world in the middle ages we can count the "Paradise" of Dante's *Divina Comedia* as one of the examples of poetical philosophy. For example, we can quote the following well known passage:
*Licht der Erkenntnis ganz erfüllt von Lieben,*
*Lieben des wahren Guts, voll Fröhlichkeit,*
*Voll Fröhlichkeit, die Worte nie beschrieben.*
*(Par.* XXX, 40. Nach Gildemeister)

continuation of life in posterity or the incorruptible names or imperishable merits which are to be inherited by the succeeding generation. Then how can we enter into true immortality? The answer is—by cutting the link with natural reality. In other words, the subject first changes itself from activity to contemplation. Then it goes up the steps of the beautiful from the material to the spiritual, from the natural to the cultural, paying attention to what they have in common which makes them beautiful. But what comes before us all of a sudden when we reach the top of these steps? It is the superb and exquisite form of the beautiful in itself—the beautiful as an independent being or the idea of the beautiful which transcends time, space and all the other relationships, free from natural reality as its substratum and which holds its ever-identical form and eternal being which neither comes into being nor passes away. The subject achieves perfect unity with its object through the intuition of these pure forms and thus enters into immortality (*i.e.* eternity).

A comparison with Socrates will show us a very interesting relation and contrast. In him, *eros* is a fellowship of life which should be established between a leader and those who are led. It aims at an acquisition of prudence which is necessary in fostering such qualities as practical, moral behavior. Thereby many discussions will arise as to the definitions of the individual qualities or conceptual determinations, but as they are the means to attain that principal objective, this conceptual cognition never seeks for its independence or superiority. Aristotle counted as one of the merits of Socrates the discovery or assertion of inductive method and the universal definition of concepts concerning the principles of cognition.[1] According to his interpretation, it was Socrates who discovered the fact that the essence of things is found in conceptual universality and he tried to acquire the conceptual determination or definition.[2] This is, however, only the sub-

---

1) *Metaphysica* 1079b 17 ff.
2) After Zeller adopted this view, it became the prevailing interpretation. It was the merit of H. Maier (*Sokrates*, 1913) to have indicated Zeller's error.

jective interpretation of Aristotle who tried to make Socrates out to be a pioneer of his own philosophical doctrine. We must put more emphasis on the fact that Socrates' intention was more practical in everything. In this connection, in Socrates contemplation never occupies a position superior to activity, and the objects of contemplation do not maintain their independence by cutting the link with natural life. Further, regarding this and his emphasis on moral behavior, his *eros* always stays within the scope of moral fellowship, *i.e.* the fellowship with real beings. It was Plato who took up the fellowship of life, which is found between the leader and his followers, elder and junior, independently from the basis of moral reality, and by bestowing the character of finitude on contemplation and its objects which have simply played the rôle of intermediary, he invented the doctrine of philosophical *eros*. From the standpoint of love in this sense, we must say that this is the proper way that is destined to be followed.

## (4)

There is another kind of love which is distinguished from the above-mentioned *eros*. It is called *agape*.[1] Historically this basic doctrine was established and advocated in Christianity and it became a specialized term, but it can be found everywhere in life. Even in our daily life, it imparts true life to all human fellowship and points to the flush of light which comes, not from the world but

---

1) Concerning the etymological or philological subjects see W. Bauer, *Gr.-deutsches Wörterbuch zu den Schriften des N. T. u. s. w.*; Gerh. Kittel, *Theologisches Wörterbuch zum N. T.* Bd. I. But it is not any solution of the problem just to examine it from the point of view of philology. It will be quite evident from the example of Plato who employed the word ἀγαπάω almost as a synonym for ἐράω or φιλέω. Nygren, *Éros und Agape*. 2 Bände. In this book Nygren presented two aspects of a typological study and historical description of the development of the concept in Christianity. In that respect this book has made the greatest contribution to the exposition of the concept of *agape*. The only defect of this book is that the author has not shown proper appreciation and comprehension of the importance of "love toward God".

from beyond it. *Eros* is a fellowship of life which is characterized by self-realization. Therefore, even in the extreme instance, which is impossible, but nevertheless a case in which we can presuppose the completion of *eros,* the subject develops by way of infinity, absorbing others into itself and overcoming them completely. As "the present" dominates everything in *eros,* perfect eternity would become the possession of the subject. As it became one with infinite being and embraced all beings in its bosom, it would experience extreme joy and happiness with its whole being. As it has already been stated, however, this is only a product of the megalomania of the self-conceited cultural human subject. The thoroughgoing effectuation of *eros* would lead the subject into a complete defeat. *Agape* takes an entirely opposite direction. It starts from an other and tends toward the self. It is a fellowship of life which has its principle and starting-point in the other. Its fundamental character is to make the other the master and the self the servant, or to change the other into the determiner and the self into the determined. If it accomplished its objective and completely disclosed its original character, there would be established a fellowship of life where the self would be reduced to nothing and only the other would be asserted. This is, however, impossible for the actual human subject whose essence lies in its self-realization. As a principle, the actual human relation is formed as *eros* and is destined to be as such. On the contrary, *agape* essentially implies transcendence from the beginning. Then does this mean that like *eros* it simply demands something which is basically impossible? Or rather is it not the true love, by which *eros* regains life or is surpassed or overcome and in which it dies and is buried, such that only then may it come to life as love and come into being as a fellowship of self and other?

Let us go further into the details of the characteristics of *agape.* Since actual human life is formed only as cultural life which is built upon the basis of natural life, it is actually impossible to apprehend pure and simple *agape* entirely free of the character of *eros,* but as *agape* confers upon *eros* a certain feature and inclination, we understand the presence of *agape.* It is, of course, a great error to think that the love between men can be established independently from human relation and therefore entirely apart from its intermediary conceptual being, but one can see the work of *agape* in the fact that it surpasses or even conquers the determinations under which these fellowships are formed and confers a new meaning and spirit upon them. This is often interpreted in the sense of philanthropy which eliminates all discrimination, or love for humanity which deals only with human existence in general regardless of any particular moral relationship. But so long as such distinctions as far and near, wide and narrow, great and small, universal and particular etc. work as the determining principle of love, no matter which direction it may take, the love non the less bears the character of *eros.* Human fellowship is constructed on the basis of humanity. But if its character is to make humanity the sole and highest principle of determination, it may after all be no other than a form of self-assertion or self-realization of the human subject. On the contrary, the first characteristic of *agape* lies in the fact that it surpasses or conquers all the intermediary principles of determination and unconditionally accepts the other as its principle.[1] Speaking from the side of the subject, there is nothing which should be accomplished by it, no need of urging it in that direction. From the side of others, all their qualities, qualifications, all the concepts of value are entirely surpassed or transcended. In any case, one can find there nothing which provides the *raison d'être* of fellowship. But in so far as actual human life is destined to proceed along the highway of activity, *agape* should always be founded on the effort of self-realization; it is determined, first of all, only by others and as far as it is delivered from all the

---

1) The so-called neighbor-love (*Nächstenliebe*) cannot be the form of the actualization of *agape* except in this sense.

fetters of intermediary determinations, it should take the form of free fellowship.

The fact that the subject is essentially characterized by the assertion of its own being and accordingly a fellowship of love can be created only in the soil of self-realization is a real obstacle to the understanding of the nature of *agape*. As Aristotle already noticed, at the level of humanity all love is basically reduced to self-love.[1] Therefore, once they devote themselves to apprehend *agape* by self-contemplation, even those who have had its abundant experience may be misled by the charm of the self-realization which forms the basic nature of the human subject and may easily overlook its special characteristics. The most remarkable example may be the case of St. Augustine who has left a great influence on later thought.[2] In him *caritas*—the Latin for *agape*—is simply a kind of—but the most excellent kind of—self-love (*amor sui*). The principal position that all love is self-love is unchanged. Simply the object is different. The object of love is the good, *i.e.* a value. *Caritas* (*agape*) is love directing itself toward the highest value, which is God or toward men as a special form of love derived from God. If we admit this view, we must say that there are only differences of degree or a partial distinction between *eros* and *agape*. Value is a condition or moment for the self-realization of the subject and as such it is a conceptual being. Thus we must also pay attention to the fact that Augustine almost lost sight of the reality or the object of fellowship. In so far as they are the objects of love, both God and man may be, after all, conceptual beings which were called by Plato *ideas*. We have already mentioned that this is the inevitable destiny of the doctrine of *eros*.

In relation to what has been said and also as a conclusion to it, we must take up the second aspect of *agape*, *i.e.* the attitude of the

---

1) *Eth. Nic.* IX, 8.
2) As to St. Augustine see my *Philosophy of Religion*, § 39 and the excellent description and interpretation of Nygren's Second Volume which was published after my *Philosophy of Religion*.

subject which may be expressed by such terms as self-resignation, sacrifice, devotion, selflessness, self-renunciation and so on. It is true that, as all kinds of love form a certain fellowship with others, there may be some kind or degree of overcoming of selfhood in all cases. Take a familiar example. In order to accumulate wealth, one may give up bodily, sensual pleasure. It is surely a kind of self-denial. But in such cases, indeed, even in much nobler and purer cases, we must notice that a self is victimised for the sake of another self of comparatively higher value. We shall find there only a relative abandonment of a part of the self. On the contrary, *agape* takes a completely opposite way from *eros*. It requires an unconditional abandonment of the self in its entirety. This, however, does not particularly mean any heroic behavior or strikingly historical incident which may indicate human greatness. Even under the simple events of our daily life or in our trifling behavior love is required as a spirit which gives life to events. That is, *agape* finds a *person* in all human relationship or in another man and takes the attitude of facing a man as a person. A person can be defined in simple terms as " that which is not used as a means but comes into being only as an end in itself," as Kant remarked.[1] In other words, we find a person when, on the one hand, the other sticks to its otherness and does not give itself up as a factor or self-realization and, on the other hand, the subject which tries to come into fellowship with it sets its foundation in the other and is activated by it and by abandoning its selfhood, lives in and through this other.

## 2. Divinity, Creation and Grace

### ( 1 )

Accepting the above-mentioned definition of the essential characteristic of *agape*, we are now obliged to draw a very important con-

1) Regarding "person", see my *Philosophy of Religion*, § 29 ff.

clusion, that the other which stands as a partner to the fellowship of *agape* should be a real other, having no characteristic of a potential self. Then it will become quite evident that it cannot be such a conceptual being as in the case of *eros*; on the contrary it must be a really existing being. But so far we have dealt with really existing others only in the sense of natural reality which stands in a natural and direct relationship with the subject. To go back to that level would be tantamount to declaring that all our effort for fellowship at the stage of cultural life was nonsense and that only the primitive self-struggle of life is meaningful. Life encounters here a crisis of great importance. Unless a new world opens up, life has no other choice than to sink into the depth of despair. Even as to the matter of eternity with which we are dealing, the solution depends entirely upon the possibility of overcoming this difficulty. In order to save the existence of the subject from falling into non-being and secure the imperishable present for it, some fellowship with an existing real other must be expected. Where can we find this kind of other? Thus we are obliged to turn to religion.[1]

In religious experience that which stands on the side of the other in the face of the subject is ordinarily called "God" and has the essential characteristic of "holiness", to use a religious term. God is something inviolable, inaccessible, completely separated from all real or so-called worldly or secular beings. And once a human subject approaches and infringes upon Him, as he asserts himself and tries to apprehend God in himself, God will show His own excellent austerity and power and throw him away into annihilation unsparingly. Ontologically, God is called the reality which takes the seat of the real other in opposition to the human subject. He is an absolute being or an absolute other in so far as He never knows compromise nor concession and stays in His real otherness to the last. As such, on the one hand, different from conceptual being which stays in a

---

1) See my *Philosophy of Religion*, § 42 seq.

possible selfhood in the face of the subject, He is entirely a true and real other. On the other hand, unlike those real others in natural life which encounter the subject directly and threaten it with its annihilation, but which are, at the same time, exposed to the danger of being conquered by the subject and always submitted to temporal corruptibility, God is a real other who always abides and perseveres in otherness. As a partner in the fellowship of love, He seems almost to satisfy love's necessary condition. Actually in religious experience the most important theme is the love of and toward God. The only problem is how we can come into fellowship with this absolute being or other.[1]

In order that this fellowship may be achieved, the holiness of God or the absolute otherness and reality of the absolute other must be claimed as such. What does this mean? It means that the human subject must be reduced into nothingness in its entirety. Whatever the end may be, the fellowship of the self and the others will be, first of all, direct encounter. Even when an intermediary is admitted, it will be an immediate agent that plays the rôle of mediation. But in this case, the third person who may take charge of mediation cannot exist. If, for instance, we take a conceptual other for the third person, it will push the subject back to cultural life and *eros*. If we take a really existing other for the third person, in so far as it is not an absolute being, the subject will keep going backwards and fall into the basis of natural life and fundamental temporality. Even if

---

1) Karl Barth said in his *Kirchliche Dogmatik* (I, 2, S. 425 ff.) that love always has its opposite or partner (*Gegenüber*), or object (*Gegenstand*), that is, one always loves the other (*der Andere*). To that extent his understanding is right. But while the words are still fresh from his mouth, in the same breath he replaces the word *"ander"* (other) with *"andersartig"* (of another kind). That is, he maintains that in so far as God is an object of human love, this object as such would be completely different in kind (or nature) from the man who is the subject and, contrariwise, that human being should be a being completely different in kind from God, *i.e.* he would be a sinner. This is a surprising and almost reckless argument. But there is nothing-strange in it, if we see that this theologian often shows a tendency to be moved by the force of rhetoric rather than logic, or by the power of feeling rather than thought. In regard to the three different connotations of "the other" and "otherness", see several passages (especially p. 23 ff.) of this book.

we put such conclusions out of consideration, after all the same problem could reappear between the third person and the absolute other. Thus the subject should first step into direct fellowship with the absolute other. He who wants to get into fellowship with God should first stand before Him. In the presence of the reverence and authority of the divine being, there is no place to hide nor any way to escape. Among current religions, if there be any which advocate a third person who mediates the absolute other and the human subject, in that case He may signify not a third person but God Himself, or otherwise He can not actually be God. That is, holiness would imply imperfection.[1] In other words, the human subject must get into direct contact with God in order to enter into fellowship with Him. But as I mentioned above, this means nothing other than the annihilation of the subject itself. When the subject is reduced to ashes in the raging flames of holiness which burn out everything, how can he restore or regain his existence or his subjective character as a center of life and as a starting-point of his activity?

## (2)

The holy that manifests itself in its absolute reality works not only as a destructive power, but also as a constructive force. The power which deprives beings of all is also that which renders being to all. In almost all religions there is a prevailing thought that god is omnipotent and everything originates from him. The concept of " creation " which also belongs to this category of thought derives from the positive side of holiness. And it will be this thought that may save us from the difficulty stated above. It is a belief which can be found widely in the religions of primitive folks or ancient people that this world was created out of something chaotic which had no order, form,

---

1) Therefore, for example the divinity of Christ, which Christian theology asserts is the inevitable result of the holiness of God.

nor life in it. And as the motive-force of the universe they usually establish god as an object of religious worship. In this case, what should be created in the universe is already presupposed as something existing. But this kind of operation should be called formation rather than creation. Here the activity of god bears the character of self-realization or self-expression which correlates matter and form and accordingly it manifests itself as activity. In this case god is represented in the form of cultural life. It goes without saying that such an expression is inappropriate for describing holiness. The absolute reality of god should take some other form of expression. Thus the notion of " creation " comes into being. This is characterized by the negation of any being or matter which might serve to stipulate the work of god. God establishes the being of others in his complete freedom without suffering any restriction or help from them and without any reasoning or mediation of others and only from the unfathomable depth of his own essence. Usually this is called " creation out of nothing " (*Schöpfung aus Nichts, creatio ex nihilo*). Originally it is found in the cosmogony of ancient religions. But later in the Christian faith it took a much purer form through the deepening of human experience and became one of her most important doctrines. Although we may already find the clear expressions of the thought in passages from St. Paul, we should say that its more theological, conceptual formulations which had the most profound influence on the later world are to be found in the writings of St. Augustine.[1]

God's love is this kind of creation, *i.e.* an act of evoking being out of nothingness. Conversely speaking, in religion creation is ex-

---

1) See *Rom.* 4:17. The former Japanese translation of this passage which reads: "…calls that which does not exist as if it exists…" is not very adequate one. ὡς ὄντα in the original text: καλοῦντος τὰ μὴ ὄντα ὡς ὄντα should be interpreted in the sense of ὡς εἶναι *i.e.* "call being out of nothingness", as ancient commentators have already pointed out. It can be found in almost all the books of Greek grammar that such usages already existed in classical Greek.—As to St. Augustine, cf. *Confessions*, XII, 7.—It is especially striking to realize that in Paul *creatio ex nihilo* is interpreted, not from the standpoint of cosmology, but from the religious experience of God's love.

perienced especially as God's love that saves the human subject from the depth of destruction. The remainder of its significance can come into our consideration, so far as it is based upon this essential religious experience or derives from it.[1] Then what sort of act is creation as god's love? It is, on the one hand, an act of reducing the other (or human subject in this case) to nothingness and, on the other, of calling it out of nothingness and bringing it into being, *i.e.* into a real otherness which exists and which possesses the center of its life. We can understand this in the following way:

In order that a true love may be established, it is necessary that the other, against which the human subject stands, should be an absolute other or reality. This request was satisfied by what is experienced as holiness in religion. In this case, the holy is the partner of the love of the human subject. But so long as love is an affair on the side of man, it is doomed to be destroyed by the very absolute other which is supposed to be able to establish it. Fellowship of love is necessary for the very being of the subject. It is only through love that it may be able to live in its original character as the subject which exists toward others and together with them. All the attempts of the subject had to end in failure, as it tried to go beyond natural life to the level of cultural life and satisfy its claim in *eros*. But now it has become evident that the last step of its leap into the stage of religion is exposed to a similar danger. In this case, it lies completely beyond the competence and power of the subject to break through this difficulty. If it be possible, the possibility should lie on the side of the other. What does this mean after all? It means that the Holy other is love or the subject of love at the same time as, or because of the fact that it is holy. In other words, it means that God's love precedes man's love and, as its source, makes human love possible.

---

1) It is hardly worth mentioning now that in philosophy as well as in all theoretical metaphysics, the notion of the creation of the universe has a very weak basis as such.

The Holy one is such an absolute reality as mentioned above. Therefore, it has no other being outside itself. If it had, it would simply be the absolute in itself. But the absolute that lives by itself and stays in its self-sameness will, after all, turn into a vanity, just as when a circle is enlarged into infinity, its center will cease to operate as such and disappear. Therefore the absolute is obliged to possess something outside its being. Now this something should be either a matter of thought, *i.e.* something conceptual, or a fact, *i.e.* something real and existing. If we were to take it for the former, no matter how we would think about it in detail (for example, whether we would think of it as something real and existing which is filled with content or, on the contrary, as something vain and empty), after all we would have to apprehend it as that which strives to assert its self-identity by means of intermediary otherness, which endeavors to realize itself in others, namely that which would be represented in the form of the cultural subject. We could say that this is simply a shuffling answer to what should remain simply and frankly in vanity. On the contrary, if we take the other for something factual and existent, we shall experience it only in religion. Outside of religious experience, the absolute as well as the other are to be given in intelligible forms. Only in religious experience can a really existing subject enter into a relationship or fellowship with another existing reality, the absolute. In fact, it is only at this stage that the absolute can have the other outside itself. That is, the question of the absolute can be raised there as a true question.

Succinctly speaking, the question may be put in this way. If that which strives to enter into a fellowship with the absolutely holy has to be reduced to nothingness and only non-being is allowed to be the other over against it, how can the subject (or we ourselves) stand before it at this moment as its other? The answer to this question will be creation and God's Love. The notion of *creatio ex nihilo* is often represented in such a way that at first there was nothingness (*mu*), then

God worked upon it and created being out of it. But if, instead of taking such a representation as simply allegorical we attribute any significance to it, we shall inevitably fall into a great error. Such descriptions of the work of God in the form of a temporal series must be put aside as inadequate. God's work is there represented in the form of cultural activity, where nothingness is not nothingness in a strict sense, but simply a kind of being or a being as potentiality or matter. As is generally known, the Greeks considered their μὴ ὄν (nothingness, *mu*) in this manner out of their thoroughgoing cultural consciousness. But nothingness is not that which maintains its own being beside or outside being, but is included in being as one of its own moments or rather as a conquered moment. The same act of the absolute other which reduces the subject to nothingness and throws it into destruction, at the same time gives its whole being, even its very center and independence. The antecedent character of nothingness which is expressed in *ex nihilo* implies that its character which comes into being in the fellowship with the other is based upon the overcoming of nothingness and thus it involves in it nothingness as a conquered moment. In other words, both being and nothingness are established all at once by the act of creation. But nothingness is simply a secondary element which penetrates into being and weakens its content. As the absolute gives the character of the subject (*subjecticity*) to the human subject by the overcoming of nothingness, it remains in its absoluteness. Indeed, we can even say that by establishing being and nothingness which conquers it all at once, and in the fellowship coming from it, the absolute also establishes itself as absolute. Once we compare this with the case of natural life, we shall be surprised to know what an important significance it has. In natural life, being implies no nothingness as a conquered element, *i.e.* it does not go through nothingness. It asserts itself directly and impetuously. Thus it dashes into others and collides with them. The beings of the subject and others can never achieve coexistence and, as a consequence, the subject is driven outside of its being and falls away. There being goes ahead of nothingness. It means that being is reduced to naught and cannot retain its own self. But now by completely reversing the order, creation saves the subject from destruction. Only the subject which possesses nothingness, not on the outside but in itself, can conquer natural life and temporality and live in true love.

( 3 )

In creation the human subject experiences God's love. Despite the fact that God is an absolute Other to the subject, it approaches the latter and encounters it, indeed, even penetrates into the center of the innermost depth of its being and recreates it entirely from the bottom. God who strictly rejects any approach of others, in a sense himself violates this prohibition and giving himself up, establishes an imperishable fellowship with others. This fellowship is mediated by no one or nothing, nor is it determined by any reasons or purposes, but it *is* an unconditional purpose in itself. The fellowship establishes itself *for* and *by* fellowship. The establishment of such a fellowship is called creation. In order to understand it, one may analyze it into several factors or elements and explain their relationship and order. But, as is stated above, such an explanation is an attempt to represent God's act as transcending all the temporalities in the examples of the cultural human life which is determined by them. We must be careful not to fall into the illusion that we can attain an objective, theoretical knowledge about the essence of God. That is, we must resist the temptation of rationalism and incline our ears to what religious experience tells us. And when we take such an attitude, we shall see that creation is not an act of the self-assertion or self-realization of God, but that it is an act of love which puts others before the self. It will not be an overstatement to say that in God love and creation are the same thing seen or named from two different angles. Even from our daily experiences we know that genuine love can not be measured by our contemplation. Even if we could elevate ourselves to the height of *agape*—although such a presumptuous confidence is, from the beginning, exposed to self-conceit and self-deception—, what first emerges before the eyes of self-contemplation is an image of self-realization characterized by activity. The love which is understood by self-contemplation is *eros*. Only when we experience the force of love in our heart and that the other is the subject of love, from whom we are loved, shall we be stricken by the holy light of the true love which can be found in human being. Likewise, not only human love, but also God's love is known to us through religious experience where we feel that we are loved by him. When we try to understand the love of God as such apart from religious experience, even if it were within the competence of human understanding, we would have no other resources than to represent it as *eros* in the analogy of human love which we attain through self-contemplation. But when we set our basis on religious experience as the canon of all understanding, we shall clearly see and apprehend that God's love is an act which is directed toward others and which gives them imperishable being by reducing them to nothingness. God's love does not start from given others, as in the case of human love, but it comes into being by or in establishing others. In the face of God " to be other " is synonymous with " maintaining true being imperishably ". This love as creation is called " grace ". It is usually understood as a love which is given to those who are not worthy of receiving it. The love which is offered to those who are equal to nothing or who should be buried in nothingness and which changes them into being should be the greatest among graces, or grace in its most precise sense. Grace is always unilateral. " Unilateral " is the right word for such love as is directed toward those who are not worthy of being loved or even have no power of loving others. We are able to enter into the fellowship of love by and in the act of creation which is given by grace.

But before stepping into an observation of the nature and structure of the love which comes to us in such a manner, let us reflect a moment on what sort of fruits will accrue from what we have understood up to now for the solution of the problem of eternity. Since we have set our foundation upon the human subject as a canon or principle, we are obliged to remain in temporality and to be estranged from eternity. From of old the human subject has tried to reach some conviction on immortality which could solve the problem of death and temporality and give ample consolation to it, by depending upon its own intrinsic power, or by entreating the power of the universe or the highest being which, as its originator may help its self-assertion in attaining its objective. Or, some of the greatest spiritual leaders of humanity have believed they could enjoy and realize eternity and immortality by sweeping away the rubbish of this world together with temporality and by ascending into a higher world in heaven where only pure and holy beings may live, thus achieving and enjoying the fellowship of love with timeless eternal being. But all these efforts and aspirations are to be answered by failure and hopelessness. True eternity can be actualized only in and by *agape*. It is only in the possibility of the fellowship with the absolute other that eternity is realized. But now such a fellowship or love can be established only through the grace of creation coming from the absolute other itself. So long as he lives in that grace, the human subject lives an eternal life. Eternity establishes itself in such an unexpected feature of life that the subject which has been entirely reduced to nothingness entrusts or gives up all its being to the power of love or of the other and thus comes to find its existence and life from and in the other. In other words, we can find eternity in and through God's love and we can enter into eternity or experience eternal life by participating in this love, or by becoming ourselves the subjects of love, indeed, even by being created into such a new being by the supreme grace. The only way that leads us to the eternal world is to give up everything to the other without relying on our own power and to become an empty vessel that obediently accepts the grace given by the other, indeed, to be driven into such a status.

### 3. Symbolism, Revelation and Faith

( 1 )

From what we have discussed, it has become clear that eternity should be sought only in the fellowship of love. But there are still several questions that should be clarified about the way the fellowship is established. How can the human subject which is made out of nothingness maintain its feature as subject in the fellowship which is the product of God's love? So far as it bears an aspect of the subject, does it not collide with the other as it asserts itself and is it not obliged to fall again into nothingness and to be ended in its own destruction? Is it not impossible to find, outside the absolute being, some other independent reality which stands in some relationship with it? Thus the subjective feature of the subject seems incompatible with the absolute reality of God.—First of all let us examine some points of question which lie comparatively close to us. As to the question whether the subject which emerges out of nothingness may some day again sink into nothingness, it will be sufficient to recall what we have said about creation out of nothing. The subject which is called into being out of nothingness is not a simple being at all, nor does it want to be as such, but embraces nothingness, into which it should again fall, as its conquered moment. Nothingness is not something which has an independent, separate being outside the subject and waits for the subject to fall into it. As it implies nothingness in itself from the beginning, the subject can escape the destruction of nothingness. The subject which has conquered nothingness never evacuates itself into a safety-zone outside it nor maintains nor enjoys pure being of itself, but it has the conquered nothingness in the center of its being, which forms its essential core. That is, if we are allowed to employ temporal expressions, the subject is always and incessantly overcoming nothingness. Therefore, as has long been said in history, the maintenance of the being of the subject is a continuous creation (*creatio continua*). But, nevertheless, even if the subject may fortunately escape its destruction, would it not be after all absorbed and buried in the absolute reality, losing its subjective character? As a protrusion from the surface of the earth is called a " mountain " and seems to enjoy its own being but in reality is a shape or aspect of the earth itself, would not the subject, which obtains its existence from and in god and lives toward god and which surrendered itself to the other, be after all simply a mode of being of the absolute or a form of its self-expression and maintain only a purely superficial, dependent or, in a word, *quasi*-illusory being? Subjecticity is essentially characterized by the fact that the subject lives and acts by and in its center. However, would it not be impossible for the human subject which is saved from nothingness nevertheless to retain nothingness at its core and to be equal to nothing if separated from the absolute? Not only in pantheism but also in the average theistic views of the world which are commonly recognized by their strong tinge of religious color, one can hardly evade this strictly logical conclusion. The god-man relationship may be either understood by the theory of natural emanation, as in the case of Plotinus; or interpreted by causality which is guided by geometrical necessity, as in Spinoza; or envisaged as a relationship between the ultimate purpose of the world and its means, as in teleological theism; or comprehended by the dialectical development of the absolute mind which realizes itself by means of others, as in the philosophy of Hegel—but in any case, to the extent that one stays in a position where one never steps out of conceptions of self-realization or self-expression, the absolute is seized as a " subject " in a pattern of natural or cultural subjectivity, and otherness is often intrinsically only potential selfhood and is obliged to be conquered and to disappear. So this difficulty will never be solved.

Here we are obliged to recall what we have said about " symbol " and " expression ".[1] According to the definitions that we have given to these two concepts, " expression " is the basic character of the act of the realization of the self; whereas " symbol " is a principle by which the subject comes into contact with really existing others. A really existing being never allows any intrusion of other existing beings and strongly resists it. If we go a step further, we can say that reality should be established in subjectivity or in the act of self-assertiveness. Therefore, if the contact of the two realities of self and other be carried out in their immediacy, *i.e.* be left to their original inclination, it would end by the destruction of one or the other, or both, because in any case, one cannot exist essentially without the other. But in so far as they are not driven to such a status and the self and other are coexistent, it is required that the other should have some link with the subject by virtue of something common to both, while it maintains its otherness and transcendence. To the extent that life is essentially directed toward others, this should be carried out in some form or other in each stage of life. It is the " symbol " which carries out this duty. But when one tries to understand the symbol by means of reflection and self-expression, he will find it to be something very incomprehensible and almost self-contradictory. But in the respect that we actually live, we find it to be one of the most fundamental facts which goes along with our living, and we see that it is the most basic principle of our existence. Our daily life depends entirely upon it. In the preceding passages where we have discussed various levels of life, the symbolic character of life has not been very clearly stated. In natural life, there was symbolism only to the degree that life might be spared from

1) See pp. 17—20.

destruction and it did not play the rôle of establishing fellowship. In cultural life fellowship was formed only with conceptual others, in so far as the otherness was distinguished from the symbolic character and simply meant self-expression, so that it was formed with real existence only indirectly. There the symbolic character of life was maintained in so far as natural life constituted its foundation. But once natural life is over-emphasized, it will end in its own destruction and in the repudiation of the symbolic character of life. Therefore, contrariwise, it should be the thoroughgoing effect of symbolism that it may save life from the crisis of her natural temporality.

We see the deepest phase of symbolism in the love of God and the grace of creation. Now among symbols, that which is most familiar to us is " word " or " speech ". It is the very basic and original form of human communication and is one of the typical human experiences that offers a key to the understanding of all symbolism. It may usually signify a stable objective image or mark or sign which mediates human relationship. This is, however, rather its derivative function. It originally has the significance that some phenomenon, *i.e.* some content of life which does not necessarily require any stable objective being, establishes a link or fellowship between men or between realities by representing or symbolizing others. Therefore, as several ancient thinkers, especially St. Augustine, have described it clearly in their conceptual formulation, creation can be called " creation by word out of nothingness." It is by virtue of the word of the absolute or God that the absolute other and human subject can enter into a fellowship. In this manner, the human subject, after giving up all its being without remainder, including not only the content of its life but also its center, and abandoning its entire self as well as its self-realization, becomes, indeed is urged to become itself a perfect symbol of the other. In the other stages of life which are based upon natural life, it is also through symbols that the link with real existence is formed, but in such cases that which becomes a symbol is simply the content of the life of the human subject and not its center itself. There the character of the subject or its existence lies outside of symbol. The content which became or will become symbol persistently keeps the character of the expression of the self. Even if they could achieve fellowship, it would be partial and fragmentary and restricted by some determination. Although by chance there may be seen some sign of the true fellowship which takes its stance in the other, it may easily disappear and only an effort toward fellowship may remain. This is the position of *eros* which is basically characterized by the sheer yearning or adoration of others. On the other hand, once *agape* comes into being, the very center of the subject is symbolized. The whole being of the subject, including its very center, is given up to the other. And its entire selfhood is reduced to nothingness. This is already an act of the other or grace. But it is not a final affair. By means of nothingness as a conquered factor, being comes forth by the grace of the same other. This kind of life which is accomplished through death and which is directed toward others is *agape* and a thoroughgoing symbolization of *agape* is called creation. If it is cast in religious expression, what God sees and wants will become what we see and want and we shall do nothing other than fulfil what God ordains of us. In so far as the center of the subject is not itself symbolized, the symbolization of the " self " contains the tendency of command or moral duty (*Sollen*), but through the perfect realization of the grace of the other, moral duty becomes a reality, what we ought to do becomes what we can do, and our life will spring out of a new center as a new power furnished with fresh content. The fellowship will no longer be a simple contact of surfaces, but will become a unity of the whole and the other whole. This unification of the two centers of the self and the other is the essential characteristic of love. Eternity is revealed only in such a complete unity of the self and the absolute other. Then there will be neither anything that destroys this fellowship nor that separates the two centers. By being supported by the grace of creation, the subject which stands on the abyss of nothingness can escape from falling into destruction and can live in the imperishable being and present. As it lives in a perfect fellowship and unity with the other, the other will become entirely its possession. By *fruitio dei* (enjoying God) St. Augustine meant a perfect fellowship or possession of the other through the realization of the self, but it can be actually carried out only by the grace coming from the other. In so far as it depends upon self-realization, a forward-step on one side will invite a backward-step on the other and the closer we approach it, the further will it recede from us. Only when we throw ourselves at the feet of the other and become an empty vessel which accepts the words of the other, will it also become our possession. Moreover, when we possess the other, we shall also possess a new imperishable self which has conquered nothingness. By the grace of creation and God's love, the subject which entirely buries its self-assertiveness in nothingness comes to life as a subject of love. In so far as it tries to be a creator of love, it will find that the love is nothing but a dream of self-conceit. It is only by giving up everything to the love of the other that love, *i.e.* eternity, becomes something real.

## ( 2 )

Self-abandonment to god's love, which is the attitude of obedience, trust and thanksgiving, is called in religion " faith ". Faith is a human answer to the calling of god's love, a new attitude of a new self which is given birth by grace; in other words, it is human love toward god. Radically speaking, faith is not a human act of self-realization, but god's act in man. This is what great religious leaders of the past have taught us. Therefore, it is the other side of the work of god along with creation, and, in that sense, it belongs to the realm of eternity and should be said to be a concept more profound and basic than those of temporality and sin. When Luther thought that faith depends upon the fact not that man is a sinner but that God is God, he had this truth in mind.[1] But this essence of faith takes some special form of development as actual human life becomes fully subject to the rule of temporality, so that eternity is not revealed in it as a simple fact. This is closely related to the fact that god's love is not revealed to everybody. Let us glance at this point for a moment.

If the love of god is simply realized as it is, a being will be revealed which implies eternity only and involves no temporality. But the actual human life is always built upon natural life and is essentially characterized by its temporality. Therefore, the secular love of this world is named *eros*, which is the realization or activity of the self. But once this root of human existence with its trunk, branches and leaves is transplanted into new soil, it will put forth an unexpectedly different kind of bud which may only bloom in the other world. This " wonder " or " miracle " takes place in the form of the revelation from god's side and faith from human side. As revelation means that something hidden is disclosed and that what is transcendent becomes immanent, so all symbols may also be called revelation in its broader sense. Existence does not embrace any other existence to himself and the other remains transcendent and hidden to him. And the fellowship of the two is made possible only by means of symbols. But as symbol lies in one of them and represents or indicates the other, so it can be said to disclose what is hidden. Revelation as a religious term, however, does not denote this kind of revelation. As the fellowship with the holy is a thoroughgoing symbolization of the whole being of the subject, so here only the interiorization of something completely transcendent or concealed is called " revelation ". In the natural or cultural life, the contents of the life of the subject

1) Cf. P. Althaus, *Gottes Gottheit als Sinn der Rechtfertigungslehre Luthers* ("Theologische Aufsätze" II) S. 21 ff.

or those of the objects are the symbols of some real others or are attributed to them as their symbols, but this symbolization is not equivocal, but has univocally one meaning. On analyzing it in detail from a logical or epistemological standpoint, there we shall find some differences of distance between the subject and the reality, and the references of the conceptual contents of reflection may gain their symbolic character, not by themselves, but by their references with more fundamental content of our experience. But these references are simply to what we have called expressions, and even in this case, the symbolism is univocal and not discontinuous. There we shall not find any equivocal fragmentariness of the content of the symbol of one reality which, nevertheless, may also represent the symbols of other completely different kinds of reality. But this can happen in religious symbols. Of course, should the love of god be realized simply as a fact and only eternity construct the character of being in its pure form—and no doubt this is what the religious subject eagerly anticipates, as will be stated later—then, all being would become symbols which directly and perfectly reveal the holy one. In this actual world, we can never avoid some degree of indirectness, that is, equivocation, which can be found in the concepts. But in religious revelation, there will appear no such degree of ambiguity, so that the one, remaining in itself, may enter into a link with the other or be expressed by the latter or further, both of them which are the others in their contents, may express some identical selfhood. Such a pure and thoroughgoing fellowship is called in religion " seeing god ". But in our actual life we shall discover the very opposite situation. In this world the divine is completely and, so to speak, doubly hidden. Here all being has the character of temporariness in its essence, so that no being can be immediately and categorically (univocally) the symbol of the eternal. The word of this world can never be that of God as such. Nevertheless, it is in this temporary life or in this secular world, that God's love should be actualized and eternity revealed.

134

So temporary, secular existence should first reduce itself to nothingness and then gain its new being as a vessel which discloses the hidden divine and eternal. But every being maintains its own original meaning and its former being so long as its actual life continues. Just as a lily in the field and a bird in the air remains, life in this world is after all self-assertion and love of this world remains to the end in the realm of *eros*. Therefore, the accomplishment of God's love should imply that while the images and characteristics of life in this world are retained, the deeply hidden and completely transcendent being should be disclosed and become immanent in them. This is what is called " revelation " in religion. Consequently, it is equivocal and fragmentary and in a word a bent, refracted symbol. To say it more concretely, the divine or the eternal is revealed in either things, men, events or history or nature. Also there may be a case that as different objects are revealed, there may appear some differences of importance, more fundamental or derivative. Although we could actually observe many phenomena which may not necessarily participate in its essence, revelation is not something which can effect a compromise or agreement by allotting fields of influence to eternity and temporality respectively (such as might be forged in the image of a half-god and half-man), but it grants complete autonomy to the two extremities. Both temporal existence and eternal being entirely maintain and assert their individual characteristics. Therefore, the object that carries the responsibility of revelation should, on the one hand, disclose the essence of the eternal holy being, while on the other hand it conceals that very essence. In short, revelation is essentially characterized by the fact that temporality and all belonging to it are not yet perfectly overcome and retain their original selves. It implies that it is a temporal phenomenon and that something ultimate should further be requested.

As we have said, the human answer to the revelation of god's love is " faith ". Faith is human love toward god. In correspondence with the equivocation and ambiguity of revelation, faith also is accompanied by some inherently resisting inclinations. It takes the forms of obedience, trust, thanksgiving and so on, but, at the same time, contains within itself opposites or at least contrary possibilities as unconquered moments. It does not enjoy such exultation of accomplished love as possessing something perfect and imperishable. It is destined to lack something continually. It is, in a way, a longing and bears the characteristics of *eros*. Although it works in its immediacy like true love, yet it seeks for some intermediary. Therefore, faith contains such moments or factors as decision, resolution or choice. In a sense, it is firmly established, but, at the same time, it is in peril of uncertainty and doubt. In other words, its certitude is intuitive, but should be confirmed by reasoning and reference. This gives it the character of belief. Thus, faith as a fellowship with reality is a practical matter, but at the same time, as an act of comprehending a certain idea or thought, it is theoretical. Having such a structure, compared with the pure love of god or the act of seeing god, the act of believing god may have only provisional and preparatory significance. In spite of that, however, faith is itself love in its deepest core and is an act of offering our entire self and being to the grace of god and of living by, in and toward god.

The thoroughgoing but equivocal, discontinuous, refractive symbolism of revelation introduces into our religious representations (*i.e.* into the theoretical content of faith) a thoroughly allegorical character. Allegory, however, will automatically disappear as temporality is perfectly conquered and love is established in its purest form. But this does not mean that the object of faith is provisional and preparatory in the field of theoretical expression, so that a more theoretically coherent ultimate expression would take its place. From very early times, the rationalists have interpreted the distinction between faith and knowledge in this sense, and have thought that the conceptual, academic knowledge of theology or philosophy could supplant the incomplete understanding of faith.[1] This is, however, an unpardonable mistake. To the degree that temporality and this world continue to remain as they are, the allegorical character of religious representation will never cease to exist. Of course, in the scope of the perfect allegory, there may be some changes and progress in expression. For example, some concrete expression may (indeed, should) be theoretically rearranged into conceptual expression. But this does not mean that the religious expression can completely avoid allegory. The eternal being is completely transcendent to this world, both in reality and in its nature. As such, it ignores all human expressions of this world. The symbol which acts as the mediator between god and man is so thoroughgoing that it leaves no room for human expression to infringe upon it. Expression comes into being only when selfhood is to a certain extent released at the stage of reflection. In temporal life, images or concepts can play the rôle of mediating fellowship, but in the perfect fellowship of true love which does not require any intermediary agent, it cannot even exist. This thoroughgoing, radical symbolism which is, none the less, put into conceptual expression, accomplishes itself in the form of allegory. God's word entirely transcends all human words. But it is the duty of religious representations to translate symbols into human words. In correspondence with revelation, which on the one hand implies perfectly human quality, but on the other discloses the concealed holy being in its completeness, the religious representations which are constructed by the ideas and expressions of this world, still deliver the messages of the other world which transcend all expressions. This is what we call "complete or thoroughgoing allegory". It is not that of a certain concept or image, but the allegorism of the ideality itself. Usually this is called symbolism of religious representations, but, as is mentionned above, it may be preferable to avoid this name for the sake of terminological exactitude.

---

1)   As to rationalism, see § 7 seq. of my *Introduction to Philosophy of Religion.*

Thus thoroughgoing allegory is closely related with temporality itself. On the one hand, it is not identical with eternity, yet, at the same time, it is identical. And the discord of the two poles is so great that it will never allow any kind of compromise. Here again we shall encounter the grace of creating being out of nothingness. As by revelation the temporal being, staying as it is, buries itself in nothingness and then gains its new being out of nothingness as a symbol, so by creation expression acquires an allegorical character. It is not by virtue of the competence innate to our power or expression, but wholly by the grace of god that we can talk about god and eternity even falteringly.

( 3 )

Faith works as love toward man. Fellowship with god is to be accomplished in human fellowship. In the world of eternity all being becomes the symbol of the holy one or of god's word. In human relationship, both " I " and " Thou " which stands as other over against " I " are given the characteristics of created being. This does not mean that the " Thou " may be absorbed in the absolute and lose their reality and subjectivity. That has already been explained in the passages where we have talked about " I ". Symbolization is the sole means of maintaining subjectivity in the face of the absolute. God takes this unique road by his abundant grace. To be created means that an autonomous being, a center of life is given through participation in the life of god to that which apart from god is equal to nothing. Here to empty or nullify oneself means to gain oneself. Now, as we have already stated, for those who have attained the human level of self-conscious or cultural being, to become a symbol of the holy one is further to become a subject of love. Therefore, under the rule of the eternal, love is always reciprocal. " Thou " will become " I " and " I " will become " Thou ". " Thou "

138

gains its reality only as a symbol which reveals the absolute reality, so as reality it participates in the holiness and eternity of god. The holiness of person or personality can be found only through the grace of creation. Further, it means also that " Thou " is created as a subject of love. Thus by the grace of love and creation of the absolute other, the holy one, the " Thou " which is love comes into being along with the love of the self, whereby and wherewith the subject also becomes " Thou " which is loved. In this way the love which comes forth from god creates and accomplishes fellowship of eternal love as well as person and personality. In religious expression, it is called the communion of saints (*communio sanctorum*). Eternity is accomplished as such a mutual fellowship between holy personalities. In this fellowship the act of the subject changes into a pure symbol of the other. A person in whom god is symbolized in pure form becomes thereby also pure symbol of another person. Thus the other entirely ceases to be an object for the self-realization of the subject. In contrast to the cultural act or activity that is called " descriptive " or " formative " the personal act is called " symbolic ". Here the subject is never mediated nor interrupted by self-expression, so that it never loses or misses the other. By and in being with god and rejoicing in him, " I " shall be with " Thee " and rejoice in Thee. To be thankful and rejoice together—this is the content of the eternal life.

But in accordance with the bilateral character of revelation, the light of eternity comes into this world refracted through the lens of temporality. The fellowship of holy love is realized only in human fellowship. Here we must omit the detail of the latter. It may suffice to have a glimpse of how it is transformed from the level of eternity. As in faith, love (toward men) is also not a simple and pure fellowship. It is, first of all, an effort toward a fellowship, yearning toward others. It must start from lack of fellowship. That is, it should bear the feature of *eros*. Therefore, it demands some intermediary. In this case, too, the mediator as such is a conceptual being. But here we shall find two ways to follow. In pure *eros*, the aim is always the realization of the self in others. There is no such thing as the inviolable solemnity of the holy one to hinder the act of self-realization. Others simply provide the moment in which selfhood would realize itself. On the other hand, *agape* aims at cooperation with the holy one. It attributes an inviolable authority to its mediator. The most typical example of such an intermediary factor is the law of the obligation to respect persons, called the categorical imperative (*der kategorische Imperativ*) by Kant, who put the emphasis on the unconditional oughtness. But not all of them have such a universal oughtness from the beginning. All the laws and orders which lie behind various, individual, concrete phenomena of moral fellowship, which determine it, define it, develop it and maintain it, and which in most cases maintain the actual powers of the subject, may be illuminated by the holy love and exercise an inviolable authority, but they may also be respected as benevolence and grace, in so far as they have constructive significance. It is an extremely erroneous view that *agape* comes into being for the sake of an abstract humanity or human being in general. Apart from concrete moral relationship or particular human life we can never find *agape* in this world. All different types of fellowship whose *raison d'être* lies in an effort toward *agape* itself or toward faith can serve as a foundation for the realization of love, only inside of or along with particular moral relationship and accordingly, can serve likewise only as moral relationships that have such particular characteristics. Monopoly of the eternal love should not be granted to just any kind of fellowship. Of course, this does not mean that we must recognize equal right and value in all actually existing communities of fellowship or in any of their concrete contents. Love which is essentially something eternal maintains its transcendent character to the last and thus becomes the source of obligation for this temporal reality and offers a standard of human judgment.

As a person (subject) receives the character of holiness, a great change takes place in its attitude. At the level of pure *eros* the subject drives itself toward a certain goal which implies some value. As it aims at the realization of the self, it seeks for others as conditions for the achievement of this end. It welcomes others, because it realizes itself in them. *Agape* on the other hand puts others first and bases itself upon others. It always finds in the other a sacred reality, a person created by the grace of god. No matter how much a true form of the other, which can be apprehended only by faith, is distorted or disfigured by the nature of this world, love maintains its original attitude without fail. One of the most typical examples of such an attitude may be found in love toward one's enemy. In the world of eternity one will find no enemy. There the others become symbols of the holy being and are transformed into subjects of love. But because of the character of this world, love is first made unilateral and then, abandoning all intention to realize some value in others, it directs itself even toward those who oppose the self. In the world of eternity, however, as the real existence maintains its imperishable, realized being in pure fellowship and complete unity, so neither conflict nor pain nor sorrow will threaten its peace and happiness. But the actuality of this world is quite different. Here the other is the natural or cultural subject who is acting against eternal love and suffering from the anguish of this world. He is the " Thou " who is always losing his being and abandoned to privation and destruction. It should be, therefore, the subject's urgent task to save " him " from this sad plight. Thus the subject may bear the sins and sufferings of the other and, sacrificing himself for the sake of the other, strive to maintain and develop the selfhood of the other, not only his natural and cultural selfhood, but his personal selfhood as well. Motherly love (*itsukushimi*), compassion (*awaremi*) or, even more, service and devotion may become the attitude of the subject or be demanded of it.—Once we live in this way, even though we are actually living in the midst of time and in this perishing world, yet we are already living an eternal life in an imperishable present.

## ( 4 )

What we have arrived at as a conclusion is that eternity comes into being in the form of love. That is to say, first, eternity is something which should belong to a subject and not to just any objective, static being. Secondly, it is a fellowship and never reposes in solitary being. In all existing, subjective beings, " to exist " is synonymous with " to act " or " to live." But all lives or activities are directed toward others and refuse to be estranged in absolute isolation. Those existing beings are maintained and accomplished only in a perfect fellowship. So long as there is a fellowship, existence can get rid of destruction. If we call the existence which is seen from the point of view of temporality, the present, the imperishable present or eternity is established only in the fellowship of love. Such life never knows want and perishing. It will be characterized by its completeness, wholeness and accordingly by the pure and spotless joy of life.

We may be able to foresee from what we have discussed about *eros* that this kind of nature of eternity was already to some extent present in the insight of the philosophy of idealism.[1] One of the principal alterations that Aristotle made in the philosophy of Plato was his identification of being with life or action (ἐνέργεια). We can also see in the later thought of Plato that he could not be satisfied with the idea of static self-sameness of being and endeavored to add some dynamic character to it, but it was Aristotle who accomplished this and placed it in the center of his cosmic view. In temporal existence, life comes into being as a movement. As a process from potentiality to actuality, it drives itself from privation to fullness. Therefore in pure actuality or ἐνέργεια there is nothing but fullness and accordingly no room for

1) Cf. pp. 102—112.

movement. But such an act is established only in contemplation.[1] The essential characteristic of contemplation ( θεωρία ) lies in the fact that what is seen and that which sees, or the object and the subject of cognition, are unified in a single form, or, if we see it from the side of the subject, that the subject becomes itself the form of the object. Therefore, it is essentially achieved in its pure form only when the subject and the object become completely identical so that they are always united into one regardless of all human effort or activities. It is manifest in god who is the pure and perfect self-cognition or the thought of thoughts. The human subject can participate also in an endless joy and happiness by associating with god's intellect by means of its own intellect... Although Aristotle did not try to analyze the very notion of eternity, he called god " the eternal " and especially, held that the eternal life belongs to god and in regard to human beings, he called human intellect (reason) " immortal " or " eternal " in so far as it participates in the intellect of god. Therefore, there is no room for doubting that he interpreted the essence of eternity as a perfect fellowship of life with the self in god or with god in man.[2] It was Plotinus who, following this tradition, tried to examine it more closely by giving a clearer definition to the concept of eternity in relation to temporality and accomplished the philosophy of idealism. Without exaggeration we may safely say that the thoughts which succeeded him were more or less commentaries on or the propagation of what he had taught. The perfect unity of the subject with the other, that is, the perfect identity which implies otherness in it was also the essential characteristic of eternity for him. His special contribution

---

1) See the passages where we have often mentioned about activity and contemplation.
2) The Aristotelian conception of eternity is so famous that it will be not necessary to cite the authorities, but see the following books as references: *Metaphysica* XII; *De Anima* III, 4 seqq.; *Eth. Nic.* X. As to the question whether the reason (νοῦς) of immortal and eternal man is personal or not, there have been several discussions in the past. Recently there was a famous debate between Brentano (*Psychologie des Aristoteles*, 1867) and Zeller (*Kleine Schriften*, Bd. 1). But the result of their discussion has nothing to do with our present subject in question.

was his emphasis on the fact that eternity comes into being in the form of life which is characterized by its wholeness or infinitude. As in Aristotle, Plotinus held that god (or νοῦς in his case) is equivalent to pure and perfect contemplation and man obtains an eternal character when he participates in this divine contemplation, this is, when he attains unity with god by this act of contemplation.

In so far as this thought has clearly indicated that eternity comes into being in the fellowship of life, *i.e.* in love, it implies a deep insight of truth. But love could not go beyond *eros* at the level of contemplation. Of course, essentially *eros* is a yearning and can be established only when there is some want or privation. Hence, in some way it should be overcome. And it is to be achieved when *eros* accomplishes its original objective. That is to say, eternity here means a perfect and pure unity of the subject with the object—pure object in this case—after which *eros* has striven, but at which it could never arrive. But as we have often discussed, can the intention of contemplation to overcome all activities really be fulfilled? If it were fulfilled, would it not equal the negation of otherness, and therefore the destruction of the subject itself, as well? Whatever is called life involves otherness in it. Where there is no otherness, there will be neither life nor fellowship with it. Then even if we accept the eternity of god, can the human subject participate in it? Of course, god may transcend all activity and temporality. And how can the human subject, which lives a temporal life and keeps acting on earth by virtue of *eros,* ever ascend into the eternal world of heaven? In god where *eros* has already perfectly attained its objective, there is no room for *eros.* There is no hand of love extended from god toward man. Here it should be man who strives for development toward god. Would this effort ever be rewarded? The answer is, of course, " No!" Such an arrogant attempt of the human subject to grasp eternity with his own hands would simply be rewarded by deception. On the other hand, a true fellowship or eternity can be established only in *agape* in which selfhood is perfectly negated and everything is dedicated to the other.

Here otherness is true otherness, that is, really existing otherness. So it never perishes and thus makes true fellowship possible. And further, for the absolute reality this otherness is not an exterior otherness which is given from the outside as a direct encounter, but it is the otherness which is established by the love of the absolute, that is, by the eternal fellowship which is its essence; in other words, even in god love does not lie in the realization of selfhood or the complete effectuation of self-identity, but is an act of altruistic other-assertiveness. So the fellowship that is established here will neither involve nor encounter anything that may ruin or destroy it. This fellowship is achieved not by the continuation of being which never sees its end or accomplishment nor by the movement which has no center of its own and never arrives at such a center, but in an act of connecting a center with another center and ever residing in that end and accomplishment. So here life or being is always in its wholeness from beginning to end. In such a being or life, we shall meet the true infinitude.

## ( 5 )

We have seen how human love is supported by the love of god. Here we must also take into consideration how our actual life and world may appear to us in the light of this Divine Love. In natural or cultural life, the other which approaches the subject is called " thing " in a broader sense, and distinguished from " man ".[1] " Man " in this case is not always identical with biological man. He should be a man qualified with a personality in human fellowship. Therefore, in so far as it is not considered as a person and is treated as a means, even though biologically it may be called a man, yet actually it maintains being only as a " thing." That is to say, thing in its widest sense is all that which a subject may encounter as the material of its self-realization in cultural life. Also the very being of man or person in its

---

1) As to the distinction of *thing* and *man* see my *Philosophy of Religion*, § 29 seq.

strict sense, implying human communication, may be called a thing to the extent that it plays the rôle of material for the sake of cultural achievement. What is usually called "human" in contrast to "corporeal" (bodily) is, strictly speaking, equally corporeal, in so far as it is considered as "material resources". Also objects are things, not only when they represent natural reality, but also when they imply beings as ideas. Thus the realm of things covers the world of pure objects or ideas. The product of cultural achievement may take an accomplished form in relation to the activity of production, but if it is regarded as staying in a state of material for its practical use, and in so far as the contemplative act involves all beings, it can be said that the realm of things covers the entire world of being and existence.

Now how will this world of things and the corresponding cultural life be transformed in the light of eternity? As eternity is revealed in love, it will clearly indicate its true being in that which is or can be the subject of love, although it may be covered by temporality. But in the realm of things this will be rather difficult. From the standpoint of human fellowship, both nature and culture may have only derivative and secondary significance of having been originated from the fellowship or having their *raison d'être* only in relationship with it. If we take them as conditions of fellowship, they are the prerequisites which are necessary or helpful for such fellowship. In any case, they play secondary rôles. Accordingly, in personality and personal love, God's love is revealed in its original form, but in the case of revelation in the world of things, its possibility itself is already a question[1] and even if we admit it, we cannot grant any more significance to it than a derivative, secondary one. After all, this is a question that should be solved by individual attitudes of respective religious convictions. But philosophy may indicate a general direction for the solution. First there is, if any, a very weak ground for excluding from the grace of

---

1) Recently in the field of Christian theology this problem was taken up as one of the difficulties in natural theology (*theologia naturalis*). See my *Introduction to the Philosophy of Religion*, § 14 seq.

god's creation the natural reality which is subject to all temporal existence. On the contrary, there is a very strong ground for including it. In so far as it comes into existence in its immediacy, the being in nature is, after all, reduced to nothingness, but none the less, it is existence. Although it may take a wrong direction, it is undeniable that there is an assertion of its existence. If there be no grace of creation working at all which, while it buries all being into non-being, calls them forth anew out of non-being, regardless of what they are or how they are, there will be found no such irrefragable fact that *they are.*[1] Thus, the reality of natural others which stand against the subject, obstruct its way and, by encountering it, drive it into nothingness, even though represented in a very improper way, may deliver the symbols of the holy one to the human subject. Likewise, ideal beings may belong to the creation of god in some form or other, and especially the ideas which, as pure objects, maintain their supremacy over natural life and strive to be delivered from it and may stand in some close relationship with the love of god. As we have stated above, this can be confidently confirmed in regard to the orders and laws which determine or mediate human fellowship, but also it may be inferred, even though it cannot be defined clearly, in such cases as in the ideas such as the objects of philosophy. Thus even the contact with the world of things may gain the new significance of dialogue with god when traced back to its original source. Cultural activity will also cease to remain in simple self-assertiveness, but will become a realization of the word of god. Once we think of the fact that human fellowship and cultural activity are closely related to each other in actual life, the latter may participate in eternity, in relation to the love toward man, as a human answer to the love of god or as a special form of the love of man toward god.

---

1) Cf. On the forgiveness of Sin, p. 153 seq.

## 4. The Eternal and Time, Finitude and Eternity

### ( 1 )

From what we have seen we observed that eternity is experienced even in this world. Although eternity and time are contradictory in nature and the eternal being remains always in a superior position to the natural-cultural life, yet the former is immanent in the latter. The same subject which lives the natural-cultural life can enter into a close relation with the world of eternity. Of course, this comes from the revelation of the love of the holy one and does not derive from the power of the human subject itself, but once it enters into the light of revelation, the close communion of eternity and temporality becomes open to the eyes of the subject. Eternity is never independent of time. Although its substance is determined by the concept of love, it is formally defined by means of and in relation to temporality. We have often mentioned the " imperishable present." This is the first essential characteristic of eternity. The present is a mode of being of the subject and so also is the imperishable present. As it has been fully made clear, it is the fellowship of love which assumes such a mode of being. The imperishable present is quite contradictory to the past. As we have particularly emphasized, the past in its original sense is a fall of being into nothingness or the destruction of being. Therefore, a perfect deliverance from the past should be the second essential character of eternity. Then how about the future? This is also preserved in eternity. In original temporality, the future indicates the really existing other. It comes into being in the attitude of the subject which expects and welcomes what is coming from beyond. As this attitude of welcoming something as or from some really existing other coming from beyond is also found in the eternal being and love, indeed, even such an attitude is the essential character of love, so even in eternity the future is preserved. In accordance with the fact that the love which establishes eternity is a pure and perfect fellowship of the lives of the Other and the subject, eternity itself is also a pure and perfect unity of the future and the present. Thereby the present and the future entirely change their appearances. In natural life which constructs the basis of the life in this world, to welcome that which is coming means, on the one hand, the establishment of the present and to that extent it prepares for some weak fellowship of the subject and the Other, but, on the other hand, it means the destruction of the present and, blocking all fellowship, makes it impossible. On the contrary, in eternity, the subject is delivered from nothingness and escapes from destruction by means of welcoming what is coming. " Eternity is perfect unity of the future and the present " or " a perfect presentness of the future ". Creation is not a simple happening at the beginning of time, as is described in the mytholgies of various races, but is an ever-happening event in the world of eternity. Where there is creation, everything is ever-fresh, ever-young, ever-living and ever-active. Eternity draws ever-fresh beings out of the endless spring of the future and enjoys the juvenescence of the present. Thus where the future (shôrai or about-to-come-ness) is completely identical with the present and rules it, there is no room, not only for the past but even for " the future " (mirai or not-yet-come-ness). As is stated above, " mirai " is the derivative phenomenon which comes into being when the future as shôrai is not unified with the present.[1] The basic meaning of " shôrai " is " about-to-come-ness " and mirai, or the state where that which is about to come has not yet come, is nothing but a restriction inflicted upon shôrai because of the intrinsic defect of natural life. In the realm of eternity, this restriction is completely removed. Here what is about to come surely comes without exception. Once one experiences or anticipates eternity and still talks about mirai or not-yet-come-ness, he

[1] Cf. p. 2 seq.

may be rather careless. In any case, eternity is not a simple negation of time as in the case of timelessness. It is true that eternity is an overcoming of time, but, at the same time, it enters into an immanent relationship with time. Such defects of temporality as perishableness, fragmentariness, instability etc. should be interpreted as coming from the failure of the unification of the present with *shôrai*. In its essence, the subject seeks for a fellowship with the Other. But in natural life, the direct contact with others which might have been a preparatory way to the fellowship causes the destruction of the subject itself. And it is called temporality. But once life accomplishes its original aspiration, it is called eternity. Therefore, time may be a yearning toward the eternal, or, contrariwise, the eternal is an accomplishment of time. As the divine revelation of God and the grace of creation which form the basis of all beings in this world are the origin of natural reality, so the eternal may be interpreted as the basic source of time. It is, of course, another question as to the manner in which time springs out of eternity. It is a question that transcends all theoretical inquiries as well.

At the same time, eternity is delivered from spatiality.[1] Differing from deliverance from temporality, this deliverance is equal to pure negation. We have seen that spatiality in its original sense is the exclusiveness of others or pure exteriority which exists between the subject and really existing others. If we are allowed to use temporal terminology, spatiality means an estrangement or disjunction between the present and the future (*shôrai*). As that is completely removed at the level of eternity, eternity in its essence is characterized by non-spatiality or spacelessness. But its internal link with temporality is still not entirely cut out. By being delivered from the past and achieving a perfect unity with the future and the present, eternity achieves temporality, as it delivers itself from it. In eternity, the relationship between the future and the present, between the other and the subject always takes the form of fellowship and, accordingly,

1) Cf. p. 47 seq.

it is an immanent relationship. And perfect immanence achieves deliverance from spatiality. We have seen that at the level of ideas spatiality is overcome in a way. But even there the spatial representation has a tinge of the allegorical. There otherness is opposed to selfhood and is retained as unconquered exteriority. But in eternity even the opposition of otherness and selfhood completely disappears. So long as natural life continues to rule as substratum, there still remains some influence of spatiality. On the contrary, as natural life is perfectly overcome and the self changes into a perfect symbol of the Other in eternity, even the last taste of spatiality will perfectly disappear. Here we see the fundamental difference between temporality and spatiality as well as the supremacy of the former over the latter.

( 2 )

We are now obliged to turn our attention from the subject-matter of time and eternity to the relationship between finitude and eternity. The two, finitude and temporality, are often regarded as two sides of the same thing. But that is not quite right. When a being has some restriction, limitation or defect, that is, generally speaking, when it is essentially related with non-being, it is called "limited" or "finite". Spinoza gave it a typical definition: partial denial (*ex parte negatio*) .[1] It is true that temporal being belongs to this category. The subject that exists in time excludes or opposes the other reality or the other subject. And as it restricts others, it is also restricted and by being the self, it fails to be the other. As a result of this contact, it constantly falls into nothingness and non-being. It is true that finitude is closely related to temporality. Is finitude, however, always alien or contradictory to eternity? In this respect, the popular view should be radically amended. From what

---

1) *Ethica*, I, 8. schol. 1.

we have discussed about eternity, it became clear that by the grace of creation by the holy one the human subject ceases to find nothingness outside itself or in the external world, but comes to possess it in its core or in the innermost center of its being as a transcended factor and then and only then is delivered from temporality and is allowed to enter into eternity. If that be so, would not the subject be eternal on condition that it is finite? If eternity is the true mode of the subject's being which, as a temporal existence, should seek for it and desire to ascend to it, it should be the true finitude or limitedness which lies in the original character or pure form of something finite in its essence. This finitude is not a simple compromise of partial denial of half-being and half-non-being, as in the case of the finitude which represents temporality, but it is, on the one hand, a perfect nothingness even at the center of its being, but, at the same time, is a being, *i.e.* an imperishable being. If we call it real finitude, the finitude which goes along with temporality should be called " bad finitude."

In true finitude, the subject resides peacefully in the love of the absolute other and does not try to seek for independence apart from it. Its selfhood or its center of behavior exclusively takes the form of the assertion of the self as a pure symbol of the Other. Its attitude is that of obedience and trust. But in natural life, although the subject is essentially finite and stands on nothingness and embraces it in its very center, yet it behaves as if it is a being and is driven recklessly on the road of self-assertiveness. This is called the immediate and natural character of life. But it means a denial of the original finitude and, accordingly, of eternity. While it seeks for deliverance from nothingness, the subject loses an imperishable being. This is called temporality. In temporality, the subject drives nothingness outside itself and asserts only its own existence. As a result, it is conversely driven into the nothingness of the outer world and has to follow the destiny of incessant destruction. Here bad finitude comes into being. That is, it is a manifestation of the arrogant behavior of resistance that the subject, which relies on its own power, tries to deliver itself from its original aspect of true finitude and, while it is created by God and is equal to nothing without His grace, tries to use the heavenly gift to become itself God. It may be clear from what we have stated, that from this bad finitude comes forth endless time as bad eternity. Temporality can be overcome only when the subject restores its own original self and returns to the love of God, *i.e.* to the home of true finitude.

## 5. Sin, Salvation and Death

### ( 1 )

Here we are forced to turn our eyes to the close connection of temporality with " sin." Temporality is a state of the subject, or a state of destiny to which the subject is forced to conform. In that sense, temporality is not identical with sin. If we remain in the framework of temporality, we shall see eternity in timelessness which is a simple negation of temporality and consequently, the only way of delivering ourselves from temporality will be to abandon ourselves to the contemplation of pure being or truth, which knows no time. It has been made clear, however, that so long as we find eternity in love, simple temporality cannot be a sin as such, although it may be a result of sin in some sense or another. Estrangement from love, disobedience toward God and revolt against the Holy—this is sin which lies at the origin of temporal existence and causes its fall from eternity and thus originates time. That is to say, the reward of sin is temporality in its perfect fulfilment, which is death.

From the fact that sin is the origin of temporality and death, it will be clear that it is not right to attribute sin to the individual behavior of the human subject. It should be sought in the original act in which time comes into existence from eternity. But as the actual life of man always bears a temporal character, this act should be something prior to time or something *a priori*. It is true that such an expression is already depending upon temporal determination and is only allegorical. As we see it in the Adam narrative of Hebrew thought or in the story of the fall of the soul in Plato's *Phaedrus*, from days of old this matter has been treated in religious and philosophical imagination with concrete descriptions and worldly coloration to aid understanding. But such questions as super-temporal fall (*Sündenfall*) are matters which transcend all imagination and comprehension and can hardly be approached theoretically. We must be satisfied with establishing some act of relaying eternity and time which will be the prerequisite for all temporal activities and existences and which determines or bestows their essential character. As this lies at the basis of individual, temporal activities, it is called by theology and philosophy " the original sin " (*peccatum originale*) or "the radical evil " (*das radikale Böse*). And so far as this original sin transcends the temporality of activity and governs even the activities of the past, in other words, in so far as to leave the present and to return to nothingness does not mean deliverance from original sin, because the self is responsible for its past, here again we find the reflection of the light of eternity as an overcoming of the past. This original sin is the cause of the simple and direct self-assertion in the activity of the human subject. As the sinfulness of the individual actions in time lies in the fact that the subject which depends upon the immediacy of this self-assertiveness refuses to be released from it and to become a bearer of the realization of love and that it takes an attitude of disobedience toward God's love, so for the finite subject the conquering of temporality should be the overcoming of this original sin.

The deliverance from sin is called "salvation." It is a return to the true finitude or to the original aspect of the subject which is carried out only by the grace of the Holy. What we call the original aspect here is not such a mode of being of the subject as can be established by its own power, but is the empty vessel which is disclosed as the self is entirely reduced to nothingness and is to be filled by what is given from the other side. In other words, salvation is accomplished only in the form of creation. Once the subject forgets its original aspect of creatureliness and entirely devotes itself in self-assertion as if it were itself a Creator, against its will it must follow the way of destruction. But what gives a new character and true finitude to the subject which is completely reduced to nothingness and makes it into a subject of love—is salvation. Salvation can already be found in this world, in so far as the natural and cultural subject is illuminated by the light of grace and shows a glimmer of love. But so long as this world continues, the subject takes an attitude of self-assertion and its life is still characterized by temporality. So long as actual life continues, sin and temporality remain unconquered. Then how can such a life show a glimmer of love? Is not that which is shown nothing but an elf fire which deceives our consciousness? Salvation of course belongs to the act of the grace of God. To that extent it is not a matter that can be argued on the basis of human achievement and status which can be known simply by the act of contemplation from the side of man. Therefore, as to the question of the manner in which salvation is disclosed in this world which is still not delivered from sin or temporality, we must say that it takes the form of a special work of the love of God and revelation. This is the "forgiveness of sin."

The forgiveness of sin should be the most principal act of divine love in the face of the fact of evil. The world without sin is the world of eternity, where there is no occurrence of forgiveness of sin and no necessity for it. There the finite subject which enjoys the happiness of love lives in the eternal present. But in so far as the human subject tries to remain in natural or cultural life and endeavors to eliminate any desire for fellowship by a total engagement in a desperate effort at finding satisfaction within false finitude, he may find neither sin nor forgiveness except as a product of phantasy. The cardinal significance of the forgiveness of sin, however, will become immediately clear once the reality of sin comes into sight. To the finite subject which by virtue of grace barely escapes the fall into the fathomless depth, sin which is a revolt against grace signifies nothing but his own destruction. Although he is facing in the direction of bad finitude, yet the fact that he maintains his existence as a subject is already a gift of grace which ignores the revolt as such. We may even be able to say that this world or this life itself obtains its existence by the forgiveness of sin. It is not such a trifling, external happening as may be granted to our particular activities. That is to say, God's creation underlies not only eternal being but temporal existences as well, which depend upon the grace of creation. Thus we are freed from the yoke of a pessimistic view of the world. In spite of all uncertainty, ugliness, annoyance, suffering, falsehood, unworthiness, ignorance, struggle and destruction of human life, life is sustained by the power of the omnipotent divine love, in the field both of culture and of human relations. It is only through the forgiveness of sin that, although natural or cultural life carries sin deep at its root, it can be a receptacle of the grace of God and that, as it steps into the realm of the true human fellowship of love by virtue of faith, it can be the trunk that carried the bud of eternal life which is revealed in the midst of time.

The only way to receive this forgiveness of sin gently and to answer to grace is to carry out one's own responsibility in his given position in this world as far as he can and to give himself up, humble himself and serve others or the public. Here even a widow's mite (Mark: 12–42) gains a splendor of infinite value. It will be the right way for those who live eternal life to do their best and to leave the rest to

Providence, but the fact that they can do their best itself derives from Providence. Thus the forgiveness of sin is itself a manifestation of eternity in the midst of time and for us the basis of all the interiorization of eternity.

( 2 )

The fact that the forgiveness of sin is a revelation of the divine love implies the super-temporal character of forgiveness and of the related phenomena. Forgiveness of sin widely denotes both the super-temporal original sin and the sinfulness of our particular deeds. In so far as the latter are temporal, they belong to the past in the face of forgiveness. But the past in its original sense implies disappearance into nothingness, so that the act of forgiving past sins, that is, the love of God, recalls being from nothingness and then conquers being; so it both conquers the past and discloses the power of eternity. This will further be made clear by the following facts: to forgive one's sin means to close one's eyes to his responsibility. In so far as one has responsibility, all his sin is " guilt " (*Schuld*) . Although neither sin nor guilt disappear by being ignored, yet there will be a fundamental renovation of the relationship between the other and the subject. By committing sins, the subject loses its relation with God and against its natural self, it resists fellowship. The grace which falls in the middle of this revolt in order to restore the relationship to the former state is forgiveness. To use a human expression, this is the manifestation of the love of God toward His enemy. Further it clearly teaches us that we must take the responsibility for sin before God. By being loved and experiencing personally the depth of love, the human subject realizes how guilty he is. So long as he stays in natural or cultural life, he commits sins simply by failure or error in the course of his self-assertion. He may feel unpleasant or regret it, but it would be an impermissible arrogance to say that he feels guilty and repents his sins. Because fundamentally speaking, the past is that which is reduced to nothingness. It would not be logical to feel sorry for what is non-existent. In cultural life the past will be somewhat overcome and will gain the character of the present due to recollection, but the past which has become present belongs to the field of influence of the subject and is at its disposal or can be altered by it. We have already seen that. The subject can further arrange it, make good use of it and correct errors and change bad luck into happiness. Therefore, responsibility in its thoroughly original sense implies something transcendent which cultural life will never handle or reach. Responsibility should be directed toward something which the self can neither arrange nor dispose, that is, toward the real other. And as there is nothing which remains in its true, pure and absolute otherness except the Holy Being, so, in short, responsibility is directed only toward God. One may talk about his own responsibility only when he himself implies some symbolic meaning of the Holy or His Word. Otherwise, what he calls his responsibility will be nothing but rhetorical euphemism or the unjustified exaggeration of the objective of his self-assertion. When something approaches us with holiness and authority, when moral duty and imperative require our obedience and devotion, responsibility can be argued properly. The sin which is the infringement of responsibility in this sense are guilt and is revolt against the Holy. The awareness of sin is called " repentance ". Repentance can be performed only in relationship with the Eternal which is perfectly delivered from temporality. In this stage, the deeds of the past are not simply arranged or modified, but the subject is responsible with its entire being. Thus guilt leads us inevitably to repentance. And that which stands against repentance from God's side is forgiveness of sin. Indeed, even repentance itself which indicates a deliverance from the engagement in sin is a work of God's salvation. It comes into being on the basis of the forgiveness of sin, or accompanies it. It is a complete error to regard forgiveness as God's reward for repentance. It is because of forgiveness that one can repent.

From this death also may receive a new meaning. As we have seen, death is the achievement of temporality and is the unavoidable fate of the subject which, estranging itself from others in solitude, keeps asserting its own self. This self-assertion is sin and death is the wage of sin. As we arrive at the stage of death, we shall realize the dreadful meaning of death in our heart. But so long as we stay in this life, death is not a reality which has come, but is a matter which we must expect and for which we must prepare. The death which we are expecting and preparing for is the only aspect of death that man can face and experience in this world. The fear of death implies, to a certain extent, the feeling of inevitableness and readiness. But so long as we take such an attitude toward death and do not go beyond it, we cannot overcome the desire of escaping death and shall never realize that death means to be reduced to nothingness or to destroy one's own life, and therefore, we shall continue to be a prisoner of the desire to live and of original sin. Only when we are ready to face death in its strict sense shall we awakened to the destiny of life in this world. Therefore, readiness toward death is the first important step in the subject's return to its original self and in its advance toward true fellowship with the Holy. So it should be said to be a form of repentance and, as it can also happen without any vivid awareness of sin itself, the readiness for death is also a gift of grace and a manifestation of the forgiveness of sin. We often talk about the nobility of preparedness for death. But it is not in itself noble to determine to die. For example, suicide as a means of escaping the sufferings of this world is self-contradictory stupidity, in so far as it is carried out under the hypothesis that death is a continuation of life. At the same time, it is a cowardly escaping of one's own responsibility. Generally speaking, a reckless suicide is an attempt to dispose by oneself of what is at the disposal of the Other and, to that extent it is a blasphemy toward the Divine Being. On the other hand, preparedness or readiness for response to the word of the Holy or the calling of God which comes from the awareness of one's own responsibility and duty is a sparkle of the pure love in answering the glimmer of eternity or divine love. As one reaches this stage, which is a step further, he will accept even death as grace. Against the background of the forgiveness of sin, both life and death are grace. What should perish perishes. This is a prerequisite for the life of what should live. This is nothing but the will of the Eternal which calls being out of nothingness.

## 6. Life after Death and the World at the End of Time

### ( 1 )

But in spite of the forgiveness of sin and of revelation of Eternity in the midst of time, both sin and time continue to exist. Although the grace of God is at work, it is not prevailing perfectly. This is not the final place for the peaceful life. Therefore, finally sin itself, time itself and accordingly death itself is completely overcome. This is the perfect realization or pure appearance of Eternity. Now we are looking at the somewhat distorted image of Eternity which is reflected on the uneven surface of the mirror of faith, but one day it will appear as it is, without interruption or concealment. As Eternity can be found in the presence of the future or in a perfect unity of the present and future, the appearance is expected in the direction of the future. It is the object of " hope " and " expectation." Now in so far as Eternity appears in the midst of time, it is an object of faith. And to the extent that it is eternal and the grace of the creation of the Holy Being, the assurance of its perfect appearance is already implied in faith. Faith is the promise of the perfect arrival of Eternity. So long as it is a promise and assurance and indicates something other than or beyond oneself, faith is hope. Every religion tends

160

toward the transcendent and thus stands on hope. But faith and hope cannot be something ultimate in themselves. They are only guides in that direction. As soon as one reaches the destination, they should disappear from one's sight. The perfect appearance of eternity and love means a disappearance of religion.

But how does this perfect eternity arrive? First of all, deliverance from time and temporality should be accomplished. At the end of time, and only through it, eternity will be perfectly disclosed to us. But this implies the arrival of death as an accomplished fact. As soon as temporality and temporal life reach their final goal, their influences are destroyed. So it is the essential character of life to look for death and to march on toward it. To attain that which is sought for, *i.e.* death, is a perfection of life, but, in this case, it is also its extinction. So long as death is something that should be prepared for, nothingness lies outside being, and life and existence continue to march on toward destruction. So far, the being which is headed toward nothingness still exists. But what will happen when it reaches the goal? As being is absorbed into nothingness, it may disappear but, at the same time, the nothingness which lies outside being and awaits it will also disappear. Here, for the first time, eternity which implies nothingness as a thoroughly conquered factor comes upon the scene. That is to say, the arrival of death as a fact is deliverance not only from life and temporality but also from death itself. It is quite reasonable that those people who opened their eyes to the light of the other world felt that a simple continuation of life, such as transmigration, was a suffering or a punishment.

( 2 )

Thus the accomplishment of salvation, which is the perfect deliverance from sin, time and death, can be found only after death or after the end of time. For us human beings who live in the midst of time such a pure eternity and eternal life is entirely transcendent. Although the eternity which is immanent in this world is refracted as a light which shines through it, it lies in the realm of our experience, so that we can give it some conceptual expression by arranging and supplementing the content of our experience. In so far as we experience revelation, we can express it in the form of allegory which not only is possible but is also allowed to us as an immediate expression of our experience. We cannot, however, experience the pure eternity itself which is to come. It is not yet revealed at this moment. If it were revealed, it should appear directly before us without any refraction, so that the allegorical expression which only is permitted to us in this world should become completely useless. Toward our actual life, it may indicate deliverance and transcendence as well as the origin and accomplishment (the beginning and end) of life itself, and so far, it may give us some clue. But the description as such is a matter of imagination or phantasy.

For many ages propheses and poems fulfilled this duty. Even theology which, remaining in the standpoint of religion itself, undertakes conceptual arrangment of religious phenomena, cannot do any more than the critical work of indicating the way of our imagination and the dangerous by-paths which may appear in the threefold character of life, as mentioned above. What is left for philosophy is to stand on a much higher level of reflection and to present a clear knowledge of the principles of the critique.

The eternity which is to come is the life after death. It is given to us in history in the form of two contradictory phenomena, the immortality of the soul and its resurrection. We have already discussed the idea of immortality. As to the resurrection of the soul, we can find it in the religion of Persia, Judaism and Christianity.[1]

---

1) Since the middle ages, the two concepts were confused in Christianity under the influence of Greek philosophy and the scholars tried to secure the Christian faith by following the argument from the immortality of the soul as it was given in tradition. Quite recently the scholars have become aware of the fundamental differences between the two. See the following books: C. Stange, *Unsterblichkeit der Seele*, 1925, S. 121 ff. The same author, *Das Ende aller Dinge*, 1930, S. 122, ff. P. Althaus, *Die letzten Dinge*,4 1933, S, 110 ff.

Their principal thought lies in the claim that the dead resurrects or regains his life. We have no time to go into the historical detail of the matter. The difference of the two seems to be whether the body is denied as an element of the life after death or is asserted or given much importance. Of course, this is a matter that should not be neglected. The importance of the body also means the importance of personality. Man as an existing subject is not entirely identical with the soul. The soul as such is nothing but a product of abstract analysis and is simply a part of man. This can be established both biologically and psychologically, but if we proceed into the notion of a person, we can confirm it with much emphasis. In order that man may live as a true existence, he should become a person. But a person comes into being only in a fellowship. The fellowship is established through symbols. And body is the scene or passage for this fellowship. The fellowship of men in the sense of persons is established by means of language in its broad sense. Countenance, gesture, eyes and ears etc. are the most important tools of personal fellowship. Personal fellowship is formed only in a fellowship of bodies. Therefore, "the resurrection of the body" means the resuscitation of man as a person. The notion of the immortality of the soul in the sense of mind comes from a false or extremely poor understanding of man. But, as is stated above, in a primitive period the soul meant rather the entirety of man. It is not a man without body, but a man with it. Only there is a different mode of being compared with that of the life before death. From the point of view of the cultured people of today, it may be regarded as somewhat unreasonable to believe in the survival of a man with a body, considering that the body itself ceases to live and act and decays, but primitive people never thought of that and were not disturbed by such a logical difficulty. Even in the case of religious men who maintained the view of transmigration and philosophers who advocated the immortality of the soul, the soul which left the body was not in reality imperfect but perfect. So apart from the differences in their anthropological views, they shared the view that the soul meant the person in his entirety. If so, it will cease to be a matter of primary importance whether our body participates in the perfect eternal being which is to come. The principal question lies in the meaning of death. We regard death as the perishing of life or the falling of being into non-being. Death is not such a turning-point of the human subject as moving from one mode of being to another, while maintaining its existence, but it is a complete disappearance or reduction into nothingness. In this sense, death is an achievement of temporality and the reward of sin, and, contrariwise, it is also the manifestation of the forgiveness of sin and the act of grace and can also be the turning-point from temporality to eternity. But if we take the attitude of evading an understanding of death as a perishing of life or destruction of being, such as we find in the recent thoughts of Christian thinkers,[1] we should be only a little different from those who maintain the immortality of the soul even if we advocated the view of resurrection. They thought like Plato that death is a separation of the soul and body and that although the body be destroyed, the soul continues to exist. As to the mode of being of the soul after death, some interpreted it as a state of pure happiness in seeing and enjoying God in heaven and others interpreted it as a kind of sleep without perception, but such differences are so trifling in the face of more primary problems to be taken up. Despite those differences, they equally propagate resuscitation into a new life of a body which had once been reduced to nothing. But in so far as the center of personality is located in the soul, this view should also seem nothing but a trifle. A certain scholar[2] distinguishes being and life and accordingly non-being and death, and maintains that death is a disappearance of life, not of being, and still sticks to the view that death is, after all, a change in the mode of being. Although

---

1) Althaus, *Die letzten Dinge*, 1933, S. 135 ff.
2) R. Otto, *Sünde und Urschuld*, 1932, S. 87.

this defensive logic sounds plausible, it is an interpretation to say that being is objective and distinguishes itself from life as a subjective being, and thus it discloses the position that life is a species which should be subsumed under the genus of being. If this were not a sophism, it might be a distortion. Of course, conceptually, the two, being and life, are different, but in the original source of life, they are entirely identical in substance. And as is stated above, eternity is not such a serene object of contemplation as is timelessness, but can be established only as love or fellowship of life. After all, we must stick to our view that death is the disappearance of life and being. Through this the solemn and grave meaning of death which covers time and eternity should be realized in its fullest form.

It is true that among the phenomena of the life after death which are given in the course of history, the resurrection is the most distinguished one, as we have seen above, but it should be interpreted that what is once reduced to nothing is newly recalled from that nothingness into being. In other words, life after death is realized only by creation. And consequently, it implies that it is the gift of grace. The radical error in the notion of the immortality of the soul or similar thoughts about the life after death lies in the fact that the human subject is said to be able to conquer death and maintain its own existence only by the power which is immanent in its essence or by the omnipotent, powerful help of the objective world or of God who stands behind it,—in any case, by his own power. If we trace such thoughts back to their original source, we shall see that they may be reduced to the natural, cultural life which maintains being *qua* being, self *qua* self, which never accepts others and refuses nothingness, and to its bad finitude and radical evil. So far as we remain in this thought of actual life, we can hardly understand that being should be nothingness through and through, and that the self should become a perfect embodiment of the other. Unless one bathes himself in the light of eternity, it is natural that he reject the notion of the being of what he cannot understand. But this impossible situation becomes a fact. It is called grace. Even in this actual life the revelation of love is just such a wonder or miracle. The accomplishment of the miracle which we experience not as a refracted ray, but as a direct ray of the light of eternity which we see with our own eyes, indeed, in which we bathe is the life after death. So resurrection is the fulfilment of creation. Even in the natural or cultural life of bad finitude where the self asserts itself by rejecting others, there was the undisclosed work of creation. By giving ourselves up to revelation through faith and love, the turn from nothingness to being comes before our eyes, though still undisclosed. In the eternity which shall come, it will be perfectly disclosed without remainder. Such an allegorical expression may itself already be following the pattern of before-and-after in temporal order, but if we take a step forward and boldly try to discuss the continuity of before and after, i.e. their identity, we can say that it does not come from the human subject, as the notion of immortality misleads us into thinking, but only from the side of God. The truth of God, the character of the Holy as a person or a subject which conquers and accomplishes everything, is the original source of the whole.

There we see the very source of the identity of the human subject as a subject or person. Already in actual life we see the identity of the subject transcending our direct experience. The selfhood of the subject can be apprehended only in and through the references to the objective content. Content is the other in the face of the subject and they are mutually others. First of all, the subject expresses itself in others as objects and then in the references to the contents of the objects. Selfhood can be found only in and through such expressions, as is mentioned above. But the self-expression (realization) is an activity of the subject and bears as such the characteristic of temporality. And activity takes the form that, as the subject lives in the present, calls the past forth into the present. The act is recollection.

Without recollection we would never be aware of ourselves and there would be no self-consciousness. More concretely speaking, in the series of A, B ..., in order to grasp B in the relationship with the preceding A, we must restore the being of A which was reduced to nothingness. This again presupposes the identity of what has been reduced to nothingness and what is being right now at this moment, and accordingly, a return from reflection to experience—a so-called transcendental recollection—and further, the identity of the subject as its basis—*i.e.* a transcendental identity.[1] This transcendental identity is, after all, the prerequisite or source of recollection, *i.e.* of the creation of being out of nothingness. As recollection determines the reference of meanings of objective contents in both empirical and transcendental forms, it is because of the latent presence of the identity which lies transcendently in the source of everything that we can comprehend the selfhood and identity of the subject empirically in or through the reference of the objective contents. This is the very character of the subject which overcomes the nothingness of the past and changes it into present being and thus establishes the intrinsic relation between natural and cultural lives, or between experience and reflection. Here we shall see, though obscurely, the revelation of the subjective identity and creative act of God. And this revelation comes to be clearer in the unity of the subject of natural-cultural life and that of love. It is owing to the identity or the truth of God as a subject of love that, while in this temporal life, we can reflect on the light of eternity. Death means a destruction of the subject of temporal life. Here life reaches the decisive stage. And the subject which arises out of this destruction, out of the center of nothingness, newly into the eternal life is the same subject which had already been dead. Already it was due to creation and grace that we maintained our existence in this world. All the more, the identity of the subject which lives again in the world beyond should be the deepest and greatest manifestation of

---

1) Cf. pp. 26—33.

grace. The faithfulness of man responding to such faithfulness of God is love. When this love which loses its brightness because of the shade of this world still shines in the present as trust, it is called faith; when it illumined the way in the form of expectation or anticipation, it is called hope. The identity of the person is not a simple quality or ability which is attributable to the subject; it is an ideal which, in this world, can be approached a little by the utmost effort from the side of man. And the effort or the ideal itself is already the gift of the grace of God.

( 3 )

Now, what will be the image of the revealed eternity or the content of the life after death? As is stated above, the religious imagination should play some rôle in accordance with the threefold relationships between time and eternity or between this life and the other life, which is suggested by the formal character of eternity. In contrast to temporal life, eternal life is 1) the source of temporal life, 2) its overcoming and 3) its fulfilment. Eternal life resides already in temporal life. Despite all the distortions and resistances which eternal life may suffer or encounter in the latter, it is already revealed and renovates the character of life. We shall strive ourselves for the ultimate fulfilment and complete purification of this effort. Of course, we must be strictly careful and critical of ourselves for the fact that our objective as such always lies in the beyond which has not yet been reached, since we are in this world.

That which forms the core of the life after death, or eternal life, is the love of man toward God and other men, which is based upon the love of God, the unity of God and man, as well as that between men, or the fellowship of the saints which consist of Creator and creatures. There will be nothing which hinders or disturbs this fellowship of love. As the self and its expressions completely symbolize the other and the selfhood is perfectly identified with the otherness, there will be neither the selfhood which needs to be realized, nor the otherness which remains outside selfhood.   Life springs from the source of the other and without any hesitation flows back to the other. The perfect self belongs to the other and at the same time, the perfect other also becomes a possession of the self.   Life continues to exist along with its fellowship and intercourse, but it knows neither interference nor stumbling nor privation nor endeavor, such as characterizes the activities of this world.   But the immediacy is, of course, not that of natural life nor that which is looked for in contemplation.   Since the days of old, the life of man toward God in eternity has been referred to as " seeing God ".   But this " seeing " belongs in the category of one man seeing another.   It should be fundamentally distinguished from seeing things.   That is to say, it means neither to see Him by means of references to objective contents, *i.e.* through intermediaries, nor to see directly by intuition, but " seeing " Him when two subjects or two persons reject all intermediary beings which both relate and separate, exclude the two and enter into and remain in direct contact or fellowship with Him.   There, not only all cultural activities, but also even faith and hope retreat out of sight and simply a personal fellowship of perfect love remains.   This is an allegorical expression.   It is true that, as in such personal fellowship, expression comes to be perfectly identified with symbol, so that all becomes clear and transparent and the subject will know everything throughout all.   Not only such allegorical expressions, but also all the thinking and inferences may disappear and there will remain only intuition, as a moment of the fellowship of love through which perfect knowledge can be given.   But even in such a perfect fellowship of the whole with the whole there still remain the differences of Creator and creatures.   Indeed, as is stated above, the true finitude of the human subject comes from this proper and clean distinction which is ever present in its authority.   And the eternity of the human subject is established only in such finitude.   But where there is neither the fear of death nor repentance of sins, where even hope and faith are left in the temporal world, finitude will be disclosed and remain as thanksgiving for the grace received and as joy in the ample gift. A perfect and pure love, gratitude and exultation--here lies the everlasting happiness of those who live in eternity.

The life after death means the world at the end of time. It is not a single being, but a co-existent being, a world. This new eternal world comes before us at the end of time, when temporal existence is perfectly overcome. As the human subject arises in eternal life through death, so the world also must go to its end. Death visits not only the subject itself, but is the common destiny of all temporal existences with which the subject shares its being. This actual world embraces in it the whole of natural and cultural life as well as all beings which are included in or related to it. Its contents are the world of men or culture and that of nature as distinguished from what is human or cultural. The hope for eternity which will be revealed at the end of time will naturally direct our attention to the destiny of the cultural and natural world. Does the perishing world really live again in some new being? The same answer that was given to the human subject and its fellowship should be given here, too. The world will end by the grace of creation, but it will be born again out of death with its new being. Of course, this can be expected from the fact that the world shares its destiny with the human subject in its temporal existence. First, speaking about death, temporality eats away even into the heart of the cultural and the natural world. Destruction and death are the fate that await them. Often philosophy has attempted to save culture from death. The most powerful and radical example may be in the conception of timelessness.[1] To explain more succinctly without repeating the details, it tries to eliminate all the elements which are related to the temporal character of the subject, as far as possible, and to isolate whatever are left as pure objects and to find eternity in the

1) p. 85 seq.

mode of being of these objects. This is just like the cultural subject which temporarily forgets its own self, escaping into the world of phantasm. Since the subject itself should always remain an existence, characterized by temporal corruptibility in its essence, such a notion is simply a vain desire, as we have explained before. Cultural content apart from cultural subject is nothing but a product of analytical abstraction and cannot retain any reality in it. The second is the teleological metaphysics which we have already discussed in relation to immortality in the sense of endless continuity.[1] Contrary to the first, this starts from the self-assertion and realization of the cultural subject, and maintains that it will necessarily overcome its temporality and fulfill itself. In this case, the subject is not an individual, but a community or, in the most typical form, human being. That is to say, the history of races or especially of human being, is regarded as the scene of the realization of culture. But although the community is far more powerful by comparison than the individual, it may be too much of an exaggeration to say that the human subject, relying upon its own power, accomplishes its self-assertion and realization in the face of the strong power of temporality. So such ideal beings as cosmic order, cosmic reason, providence etc. are introduced as aids. They may secure timeless being as ideas or pure forms, in so far as they are separated from the selfhood of the subject, but as simple objects they have, of course, no real power in and of themselves. Therefore, they are obliged to be granted some reality of their own. But as the famous word of Hegel teaches us, substance (*Substanz*) should become subject (*Subjekt*). The Other which has to be a helper of the human subject is thus lifted to the throne of the absolute subject. This is the god of metaphysics in philosophy. Now in order that such a god may be a true protector of culture and a dynamic source of the self-realization of the human subject, it should be not only a blind power of the assertion of the self in the sense of the subject of natural life, but also a subject in the sense of the cultural subject, which accomplishes itself

---

2)  pp. 75—84.

in and through the conceptual content. It may be distinguished from the human subject by such honorable titles as infinite, absolute etc., but the content of its life and its self-realization will be nothing but that of human culture itself and only it may be granted some superiority in its mode of being. Even if it may also be considered as a kind leader who gives cultural content to men, or even if it may be represented as an absolute subject who expresses and realizes itself in the history of human culture, fundamentally it is like an enlarged portrait of the human subject. The real force for overcoming temporality and its inevitable result, death, is not granted to such a subject. Thus the source of its real power will not be sought for in the character of the subject but in the content of pure objects or of ideas which maintain their own pure beings before entering into a temporal relationship, and in their timelessness. Thus the *Idee* which occupies the seat of substance in opposition to God or the Absolute Mind, *i.e.* the Absolute Subject, and which is eternal only in the sense of timelessness—this *An sich* in opposition to *An und für sich*—should become the source of its real power. As such, *Idee* may also be equipped with the character of the subject and may realize itself, but after all it is only an idea of the subjectivity, a self-realization of an idea, and this ideal world which might be interpreted as the unveiled form of god which precedes the appearance of the finite being, may be no other than a simple " land of a shade " (land of phantoms). The attempt to grant its own eternity and deliverance from death by its own power to culture and its history will all be ended in failure. Human culture and human history should end and be drowned in the abyss of death and destruction as time comes to an end.

Then what would nature be? What we call nature here stands in a close relationship with the natural life which we have called the primitive and fundamental level of life, but they are not entirely identical. It is the name ordinarily given to all that cannot ascend to the level of the cultural subject in the world of existing reality, that is, to the totality of all the existing realities excepting human being. The contact with it is carried out, of course, first in natural immediacy, but the really existing other is characterized by the fact that it never steps out of it and goes into human fellowship. So far as it deals with culture, it plays the rôle of matter. Unless it is considered as a cultural, moral subject, or so long as it is contemplated in its natural or objective reality, the human subject belongs to nature. We get contact with nature through her immediacy and experience some content as her symbol, but this content is exalted to the object at the level of reflection, and further it is attributed to the existing other and thus nature and her cognition are established as the objective world of reality. In that case, that which can be uplifted to reflection and cultural being is only the subject and the other stays on in the stage of natural reality. Therefore, nature is a realm where there is no freedom, but compulsion and necessity. Temporality and spatiality are her most fundamental characteristics. It is quite natural that this nature should be reduced to nothingness together with temporality. It is also because natural life forms its basis that the cultural world cannot escape the destiny of death and so far as nature encounters the subject in its natural life, the entire nature except man should follow the way of destruction together with culture, carrying all its elements as well as all their relationships.

Thus the world will perish, but it does not remain perishing. It will revive in new being. This is the work of the grace of creation which calls being out of nothingness. As in the case of the fellowship of persons, here again the revival means perfection. That is to say, all is created anew, but at the same time the identity is preserved. And ultimately this identity depends upon the identity or the truth of God as the subject of love. Everything in this world goes under the ever-flowing Lêthê (forgetfulness) at the end of time, and passes into the past. Its rebirth from nothingness into being does not depend upon the power of this world or its memory. This world is reduced to nothingness. Only the truth of the fundamental recollection of God, which is his personal identity as the subject of love, can achieve this miracle. It is almost beyond our imagination what is the content of the new world which is free from all temporal impurity and shines in the light of eternity. We can only say the following: Even in this world, wherever the light of love shines, even the cultural activity whose essence lies in its self-realization meant an achievement of the word of God. Even natural reality which forms the basis of all being became a symbol of the eternal reality. This will be thoroughly effectuated and accomplished in the world beyond. The blind resistance of nature will change into the dignity and glory of God. The arts and sciences of this world will perish, but can anybody deny that the word of God will fill our ears and eyes in eternity with its inexplicably beautiful and pure form and sound? In this world, ideas have authority in proportion to the excellence of cultural life. In the other world where love and eternal reality is the unique being, the holy recollection of God may grant revival first to those concrete individual contents which were neglected in this world. The human fellowship of this world may cease to exist in the other world. But those who have already delivered the divine message in this world may speak the same word more clearly and strongly in the other world. Sometimes the popular belief that we may be able to meet again in the other world is simply depreciated as groundless superstition. But who can flatly deny that such an attitude comes from the over-estimation of the wisdom of his world and is an act of camouflaging the truth of God?

In short, in the coming world, both the men and the things of this present world and their fellowship may cease to exist as they are now. But their content (the content of culture and the content of nature) will be saved from perishing when it is restored from nothingness to being through the Eternal's recollection and it will create and enrich the eternal love which is all and embraces all, as well as an imperishable life which links man with God and man with man.

# Translator's Note

As is the case with other translations of Japanese philosophical works, that of Dr. Hatano's *Time and Eternity* brought forth several discoveries (such as the two distinct concepts of future in Japanese: *shôrai* and *mirai*) as well as some difficulties. Here I would like to limit myself to an attempt to make clear to Western readers the causes of the latter in connection with Hatano's philosophy which are created by the structural differences between Japanese and English.

There are certain *lacunae* in the Japanese language which cause some ambiguities and obscurities of meaning, even to Japanese readers. Several determining factors such as articles (a, the), number (singular, plural) and large and small letters which are found in most of the Western languages are missing (or, not expressed, even when they are not missing). So a word, *tasha,* may be translated into "other", "others", "an other", "the other", 'the Other" etc., depending uopn the context of individual circumstances, while it is much clearer in German or Latin for example, where even the determinations of gender such as "other man" (*der Andere, alius*) and "other thing" (*das Andere, aliud*) can be morphologically distinguished.

These wants are rather fatal in making analytical statements in which the most clear and distinct use of terms is required both quantitatively (*e.g.* in number) and qualitatively (*e.g.* in gender and person). Especially the lack of gender in Japanese nouns creates a particular difficulty in expressing such a personalistic view of theology as Hatano's tripartite schemes where the impersonal aspects of the natural life of desire (ἐπιθυμία) and the cultural life of *eros* ( ἔρως ) are sharply distinguished from the personal aspect of the religious life of the fellowship of love ( ἀγάπη ). (About the distinction of *thing*

175

and *person,* see *Time and Eternity* p. 42 ff.)   As a result, the style of *Time and Eternity* is obliged to bear the neutral or impersonal tinge of philosophy of religion instead of theology, although its content is filled with a personalistic analysis of the types of love in which one lives.

Moreover, the obscurity is accentuated by the equivocal connotations of *kanji* (Chinese characters) which have long been employed to express abstract ideas in Japanese language and have been used by the pioneers of the study of Western philosophy for translation since the second half of the last century.   They have been established in modern Japanese philosophy as her instruments for expressing those concepts which are purely occidental, sometimes without entirely losing their traditional Confucian or Buddhistic overtones.

In the third place,—and this is most important from the point of view of philosophy—one thing that may puzzle Western students of the Japanese language is the frequent omission of the subjects in the sentences.   The English answer to a question: " Do you go to school today?" may be either: " Yes, *I* do." or " No, *I* don't." where the subject of the sentence, " I ", is never omitted, whereas the verb can be. Quite contrariwise, in Japanese conversation, the same question may be answered by *" Yukimasu "* (" Go ") or *" Yukimasen "* (" Not-go ") in which the statement of the subject is not made, unless it is strictly necessary, although the verb which refers to the state or action of the subject is simply repeated.   And it happens not only in colloquial conversation, but also in more formal or literary phrases such as in the writings of philosophy.   This is one of the most peculiar phenomena of this language.   In Latin or Greek in which subjects are not always stated, the conjugation of the verbs indicates quite clearly whether they represent first, second or third person, singular or plural. In Japanese, even to express subject by conjugation is impossible.

Then in what manner is the notion of the subject constructed in Japanese?   What is the rôle of those *quasi*-subjects which are expressed by such suffixes as " *-wa* " or " *-ga* "?   They appear once or twice in the introduction of the subject-matter and then disappear almost completely in the succeeding passages. It seems that in Japanese the subject signifies a place or seat (*locus*) where a state or action happens. Once this *locus* is stated and made clearly *under-stood,* it is no longer necessary to be cited again. In that sense, the subject in Japanese sentence may be said to play the most orthodox and traditional rôle of *subjectum* (lying-under or situated-below) or *substratum* (spread-beneath) in Latin upon which or to which something or some event happens or by which happenings are propped or carried. An event, " going ", happens (*accidit, contingit, evenit*) to, or is carried by, the subject, " I ". It is not that an " I " makes a decision of going to school, but it is a phenomenon, " going-to-school ", which *happens to* or is *propped by* the subject, " I ".

$$Yukimasu = \frac{\text{``Going-to-school''} \ (Phenomenon)}{\text{``I''} \ (Subjectum)}$$

This is what Aristotle called ὑποκείμενον which *underlies* the accidents (πάθη, συμβεβηκότα). And this will also explain the curious juxtaposition of subjects in such a sentence as " *Watashi-wa* (I) *atama-ga* (my head) *itai* (aches) ." Actually it should denote: An aching is happening to the subject, " I ", particularly to " my head."

In modern languages of the West, it is almost impossible to construct a sentence without a subject, except in an imperative sentence, where the object of command or prohibition, " You ", is understated. As it may be easily discovered, this omission of the subject adds further vagueness to Japanese philosophy which is already affected by the esoteric Chinese characters and by the lack of determining elements. And it is not only philosophy which is affected by this linguistic vagueness, but also average Japanese thinking is more or less influenced by this neutral impersonal character. The notion of responsibility is often submerged in an anonymous set-up of impersonal competency (or incompetency) of political institutions. The militant spirit of unionism is easily masked by the unidentifiable flux of the masses. Such traditional terms as *sabi* (elegant simplicity), *wabi* (quiet taste) or *shibusa* (sober, quiet and refined taste) implicitly convey the trend of impersonalization. The notion of nothingness (*mu*) seems to be linked with the complete deletion of the subject or the thinking, willing self, which is to be reduced into natural being as such.

In this respect, Hatano belongs entirely to the West, although his attire is of the East. It was his great contribution to the philosophical minds of Japan that he tried to analyze the structure of the long-neglected " human person " or " subject " which has been hibernating under the impersonal climate of the poetry of undifferentiated *mu*, where such conceptions as the responsibility of the subject or the awareness of sins are often veiled by the neutral impersonalization of " it " instead of " I ".

In this connection, it would be worth mentioning how the term *shutai* (subject) obtained its new rôle of philosophy in Japan. According to the original usage in the *Book of Han* which was written in the first century after Christ in China, *shutai* meant " body of emperor " who exercised his will over the subject. In the beginning of this century when the Japanese academic activities were gradually organized, the notion of *shutai* was first adapted in jurisprudence to denote the subject of legal right or obligation which exercises its will and action to others. Formerly when the influence of the Neo-Kantian School (under which Hatano started his philosophical career) was strong, a word " *shukan* " was used as the translation of German *Subjekt*. It was in the philosophy of Kitaro Nishida (1870–1945) that the word *shutai* gained its special meaning in philosophy. In contrast to *shukan* (literally, subject of contemplation) which has the epistemological connotation of super-individual, formal, pure consciousness as such, the *shutai* (literally, master-body or subject of experience) has an ontological and ethical sense of an existence furnished with consciousness *and* body, an individual subject responsible for its own behavior. It was in the epoch of the decadence of the Neo-Kantian School just before the

Second World War when the defect of the Kantian formalism was cited, that the epistemological study of *essentia* had to be turned into the study of a living, existing subject, *existentia*.

It is interesting to notice that the same effort has been made also by German and American thinkers rather recently. As Carl Michalson notes in his *Japanese Contributions to Christian Theology* (1960, p. 33), "subjective" in English can mean "either a state of private feeling or an intimate personal encounter with a reality outside oneself." For the former, Nishida, Hatano, Nishitani etc. use the word *shukanteki*; for the latter, *shutaiteki*. The suffix, *-teki*, converts the nouns, *shukan* (subject of contemplation) and *shutai* (subject of experience) into adjectives. Martin Heidegger has recently invented a verbal distinction that serves the same purpose in his *Holzwege* ("Nietzsches Wort 'Gott ist tot'", 1950). The German term *Subjektivität* was always subject to the same equivocation as its English equivalent *subjectivity*. Therefore, *Subjektität* was created to bear the special meaning that the Japanese *shutai-sei* connotes. Michalson translates it *subjecticity*.

It is not my duty here to step into the detail of Hatano's thought and to describe the way he distinguishes the time of human experience from impersonal objective time. Suffice it to say that he was quite successful in carving out the "subjecticity" of the subject. But alas he was obliged to fulfil his task with a language which has the deficiencies mentioned above and tends to create a dimness of meaning with its neutral wording.

On the other hand, as he declares in the preface, the fact that he stands on the footing of the philosophy of religion, not that of theology, prevents him from employing more theological expressions of Christian faith. This is not surprising if one remembers that he was a professor of "Religious Studies" at the University of Kyôto. Japanese government schools have no independent faculty of theology. There the study of religion is comprised of two fields, *i. e.* the phenomenological study of various religions and the philosophy of religion. As the head of the section of religious studies where Shintoism, Buddhism and Christianity are evaluated in parallel with the philosophy of religion, he could not confine the academic study on Christianity within a certain theological doctrine which stands upon a particular ecclesiastical background. Accordingly, he was obliged to employ neutral terms and styles in his writings and lectures. But as Professor Kazuo Muto also expresses the thought in his *That which lies in between Theology and Philosophy of Religion* (1961), it was Hatano's view that the academic study of Christianity should not be restricted by the point of view of a certain theology, but be freed to wider perspective of reason in the religious study (*Religionswissenschaft*) or the philosophy of religion (*Religionsphilosophie*). Because of this, I have left several important words in small letters which are usually written in capitals in Christian tradition, such as the Being, God, the Divine, His, the Eternal etc. with the exception of those places in the last chapter where evidently he stands on Christian theology.

These are the excuses for many awkard, unidiomatic and unorthodox sentences which are found in my translation. As we shall easily see from the list of the quotations and foot-notes, Dr. Hatano's writing is based upon his wide and extensive reading of the philosophical and theological works of the West (especially of Germany). His attitude was of highly scholarly accuracy. His knowledge was not only wide and broad, but also very profound even in the field of Greek and Latin languages. But in spite of this ample intellectual capacity, he expresses himself in quite a modest and abridged style. This is also another difficulty which the translator had to face from the beginning. But as the key to the solution may be given in the introductory preface, so my remarks here are restricted to explaining simply the linguistic difficulties of the translation of Japanese thought into English. I dare to hope that the points which are stated here may stimulate the interest of both Japanese and foreign scholars in the analytical study of Japanese language as the instrument of philosophy and theology (which has not been very seriously undertaken up to now).

My grateful acknowledgements are due to Dr. Ken Ishiwara of Aoyama Gakuin University and to Mr. Yoichi Kôno, former professor of Tôhoku University, for valuable advice in the technical problems of the translation and to Dr. Carl Michalson of Drew University with whom I had the privilege of reading the entire text of *Time and Eternity* when he was in Japan during the spring semester of 1958 and who kindly accepted this time the bothersome work of the critical reading of the whole translation and to my friend, the Rev. John Krummel who also read the manuscript and has made many helpful suggestions, corrections and criticisms.